DREAMERS

& DOERS

DREAMERS
& DOERS

Inventors Who

Changed Our World

by

Norman Richards

Atheneum · *1984* · *New York*

INTRODUCTION

THE PROGRESS of our country can be measured in a long series of inventions over the past two centuries. These inventions have made it possible for this nation to produce the goods that people need and to create industries and jobs so people can earn their living. They have provided us with modern communications, with fast, safe means of travel, and with the ability to explore far beyond our world. They have given us the medical means to eliminate many diseases and to cure sickness in millions of people. And they have given us new products to make our lives more convenient and comfortable than our ancestors ever dreamed possible.

The inventors who provided all this for us— and who are still working to make our lives better— were and are remarkable people. History shows that they have had some special qualities that enabled them to make their dreams come true. Some came from backgrounds of poverty and little education, while others have been highly educated. Some did poorly in school while others were brilliant students. But most of them have had certain qualities in common. Each had a dream or vision and clung to it

stubbornly. And nearly all of them faced discourage-
ment and failure at times in their careers. Rather
than give up, they learned from their failures and
went on trying until they succeeded.

This book describes the lives and achievements
of four of these remarkable inventors: Robert Goddard, Charles Goodyear, Thomas Edison and George
Eastman. They are members of a select group who
have been honored by induction into the National
Inventors Hall of Fame. The Hall of Fame was established in 1973 by the National Council of Patent
Law Associations and the Patent and Trademark
Office of the U.S. Department of Commerce. It is
administered by the National Inventors Hall of
Fame Foundation, a nonprofit institution.

The National Inventors Hall of Fame is dedicated to the individuals who conceived the great
technological advances that this nation fosters
through its patent system. The purpose of the Hall
is to honor these inventors and bring public recognition to them and to their contributions to the
nation's welfare.

Inventors are selected for the Hall of Fame by
a selection committee composed of representatives
from national scientific and technical organizations.
Each year the members of this committee vote to
select the most qualified inventors from those who
are nominated for induction.

At the time this book was printed, fifty-three
inventors had been chosen for the Hall of Fame. It
is a high honor, indeed, to be selected. Few, if any,

could be more deserving than the four men whose lives are profiled in this book. Their vision, their talent and their persistence in the face of great challenges should serve as an inspiration to everyone.

Norman Richards

Inventors in the National Inventors Hall of Fame

Edwin H. Armstrong
Ernst Alexanderson
Andrew Alford
Luis Walter Alvarez
Leo Hendrik Baekeland
John Bardeen
Alexander Graham Bell
Harold Stephen Black
Walter H. Brattain
William M. Burton
Wallace H. Carothers
Chester F. Colson
William D. Coolidge
Lee deForest
Rudolph Diesel
Carl Djerassi
Herbert Henry Dow
Charles Stark Draper
George Eastman
Thomas A. Edison
Philo T. Farnsworth
Enrico Fermi
Henry Ford
Jay W. Forrester
Robert H. Goddard
Charles Goodyear

Charles Martin Hall
James Hillier
Charles F. Kettering
Jack S. Kilby
Edwin H. Land
Ernest Orlando Lawrence
Theodore H. Maiman
Guglielmo Marconi
Cyrus McCormick
Ottmar Mergenthaler
Samuel F. B. Morse
Robert N. Noyce
Nicholaus August Otto
Louis Pasteur
Charles J. Plank
Edward J. Rosinski
Lewis H. Sarett
William B. Shockley
Charles Steinmetz
George R. Stibitz
Nikola Tesla
Max Tishler
Charles H. Townes
Eli Whitney
Orville Wright
Wilbur Wright

Vladimir Zworykin

ROBERT H. GODDARD

---

*The Father
of Modern Rocketry*

A FAMOUS saying goes: "There is one thing stronger than all the armies of the world, and that is an idea whose time has come." Indeed, the right idea at the right time can have a force that will overcome all obstacles and change the world. Yet for Robert H. Goddard's idea—space travel powered by rockets—the time had not come. This great American scientist waged a lonely, lifelong fight for his dream of rocket power in the first half of this century; he received little support from the public or the government. Had America supported his work during the 1920s and 1930s, we might have developed such powerful military rockets that our enemies would have been afraid to start World War II. We might have been prepared to enter the Age of Space twenty years sooner than we did.

Man's trips to the moon, the space shuttle and other accomplishments in space have been conducted by teams of scientists and vast sums of government money. Yet the success of these missions has been based on the knowledge and the experiments conducted many years earlier by a dedicated man who had to "go it alone" in his experiments with limited money from private sources. Today's space scientists acknowledge that Robert Goddard was the "father of modern rocketry"—the man whose ideas made space travel possible.

Who was this remarkable man? Born in Worcester, Massachusetts, on October 5, 1882, Robert Goddard showed a great deal of curiosity about how things work when he was a child. He was frail and couldn't keep up with other boys in running, jumping, and sports. So instead, he became an avid reader. His favorite reading was books and articles about space travel by such authors as Jules Verne and H. G. Wells. He would sit for hours reading and rereading Verne's book *From the Earth to the Moon,* noting where the author's fiction wasn't factually correct and writing the correct facts in the margins. He especially liked the parts where the author described the preparations made for the trip to the moon. He would study these with excitement, trying to reason out the actual possibilities for such a mission.

Over a period of months, a newspaper called the *Boston Post* published a series of articles called, "Fighters from Mars or the War of the Worlds, In and Near Boston." The articles described a space flight from Mars to Earth and an invasion of Boston by Martians. Young Bob Goddard found this exciting reading, too, and it made him all the more curious about the possibility for actual space flight.

He had a burning need to know and to find out things for himself. He was forever experimenting. When he was only five, he had seen electricity produced by a battery in his uncle's workshop. He also noticed that he could make electric sparks by scuffing his feet along on a carpet. Putting these facts together, he decided to rub zinc from the battery on his shoe soles and try to produce a big spark which would lift him off the earth. His mother soon put a stop to the experiment, but it didn't dampen his curiosity.

Using his bedroom as his "laboratory," Bob conducted experiments throughout his childhood. In one project, he made a balloon out of sheet aluminum, welding the sheets together so that it formed the shape of a pillow. He persuaded a local druggist to fill the balloon with hydrogen and attempted to launch it on the end of a long string. But the aluminum sheets were not thin enough—the balloon had too much weight for the hydrogen to lift.

Some of his other experiments resulted in blasts that blew out windows in his "laboratory." He was experimenting with a mixture of hydrogen and oxygen to see if he could produce a force that would lift an object in the air; he found out, to his dismay, that such a mixture must be handled very carefully.

Fortunately for Bob, his parents took an interest in his scientific ability and encouraged him in his

[5]

experiments. His father told him that although most people considered the idea of rockets and space travel silly, he didn't. He said he knew Bob would want to work toward the goal of space travel, but that he would have to prepare himself with a good education. "You can't reach your goal with haphazard experiments," he told him. "You need to study math and science, because true scientific work depends on these tools."

Although Bob loved the study of physics, math was difficult for him. But he studied hard, because he knew it would be important to the career he hoped to have. During high schoool, he continued to "invent" novel ways to propel objects into space. He wrote an article titled "The Navigation of Space" and submitted it to *Popular Science News,* but it was not published. He tried other articles, but the result was the same. The problem was that his reasoning in these articles was not based on scientific principles.

"By the time I graduated from high school," he wrote later, "I had a set of models which would not work and a number of suggestions which, from the physics I had learned, I now knew were erroneous. Accordingly, one day I gathered together all the notes I could find and burned them in the little wood stove in the dining room."

But he was far from discouraged. He went out and bought a new set of notebooks and continued his habit of entering his thoughts and observations in them every day. He continued this habit throughout his life.

As he studied the sciences in high school, Bob discovered that each field of science depends on others. You need to know chemistry to understand physics, and vice versa. Engineering depends on mathematics, and so on. He even found that physiology could be useful. When he learned that the human body depends on a small structure in the inner ear for its sense of balance, he began to think about how a bird maintains its balance in flight. After studying this system, he tried to build a mechanical system that would do the same thing. He was thinking that some day a rocket would need a balancing device to tell if it was on course. The project was a failure, but he learned a bit more about flight.

Not long after this, he had another idea for control during flight. He remembered the unusual way a toy called a gyroscope top works. If you start such a top spinning and moving in a certain direction, it will continue that way, even if you try to interrupt it. If you try to push it over, and it is spinning with enough force, it will right itself and continue on as it had been.

At first, Bob had thought of using this stubborn force as a means of *propelling* a rocket, but it proved to be too small to be effective. But he recorded the experiment in his notebook anyway, for possible use later. And indeed, the gyroscope experiment did turn out to have the seed of a very good idea later.

[7]

He thought about using a combination of gyroscope devices, perhaps set up at right angles to each other. Such a combination might be used to "report" conditions that tried to push the gyroscopes (and the rocket) off course. Maybe the resistance that the gyros produced would be strong enough to make some mechanism work to put the rocket back on course. He filed the idea with other thoughts that might be used some day.

Although Bob seemed preoccupied at times with his dreams of rocket ships in space, he found time for a number of other interests in high school. He edited the school paper, sang and acted in school shows and plays, and was elected president of his class. Most of his classmates regarded him as a "brain" who would probably do well in science, but they weren't sure where. Bob wasn't sure himself. He was told that his dream of rockets and space travel was impractical, because there was no such science or industry at the time. Rocketry was only a haphazard "pseudoscience" or "fake science" in 1904, when he graduated from high school.

It's true that the Chinese had made crude rockets about nine centuries before, and that they had been used for military purposes since then. But they were small devices with little power and limited range. Mostly they were used to light up the sky at shows and celebrations—the kind you see at Fourth of July fireworks displays. But by the time Robert Goddard's career ended in 1945, he had helped make rocketry a full-fledged science, using the knowledge of physics, chemistry, astronomy and engineering.

In his high school years, however, he was told that there were no full-time jobs inventing rockets and that he'd better prepare for other jobs in science, such as teaching. Bob agreed to do this, and he became a student at Worcester Polytechnic Institute, a college of engineering and science. But even as he studied such courses as physics, he kept seeing how the principles of science could be applied to his dream of building rockets. One of the principles he learned in physics is called Newton's Third Law. This scientific law states that *for every action there is an equal and opposite reaction.* An example of this principle would be the use of a fire hose. When a fireman is holding the nozzle of a hose and water is rushing out of the hose under great pressure, he has to *react,* or fight back against the hose. The water rushing out of it in one direction pushes the nozzle in the opposite direction. It is this principle that is at work in today's jet engines. Hot air and gasses rushing out the rear of a jet engine push the airplane in the opposite direction. The principle applies to rockets as well as jet engines, and Robert Goddard's study of it is one of the main reasons we have successful jet travel and space missions today.

Even though his experiments had been failures and people considered rocketry silly and impractical, young Bob Goddard felt sure that the reaction principle would someday permit man to take rocket ships into space. "I began to realize that there might be something after all to Newton's Laws," he wrote later. "The Third Law made me realize that if a way to navigate space were to be discovered or invented, it would be the result of a knowledge of physics and mathematics . . ."

He studied hard at Worcester Tech, as the school was called, because he was now getting the advanced scientific training he would need. But he also found time for other interests, as he had in high school. He was editor of the school paper, class president, and even wrote the school song.

Still, he never left his main interest for long. He wrote a paper on the use of atomic energy, predicting that the energy from nuclear substances would someday power rockets into space. But one of his professors told him that the idea wasn't practical, and this discouraged him for a time. However, he soon reacted as he usually did when faced with failure—he vowed to "pick up the pieces and keep trying." In 1907, in his junior year at the college, *Scientific American* published an article he had written on the use of the gyroscope for balancing airplanes in flight.

He graduated with high grades in 1908 and hoped to study for advanced degrees at Clark University, which is also in Worcester. But his parents didn't have enough money to pay his tuition at the time, so he accepted an offer of a teaching job at Worcester Tech. He taught for a year, saving his money to enter Clark, and he was finally accepted.

After two busy years there, he received his doctorate in 1911.

Next he went to Princeton University in New Jersey on a one-year research fellowship. His job there was to do research in the Princeton laboratories, but the work he did was not related to rockets. He worked each day in the lab, waiting for evening when he could concentrate on his own interests—mathematical plans and calculations for rockets. He often worked far into the night, sometimes until dawn. He was excited by this study, because he was proving, on paper at least, that reasonably small amounts of fuel could lift rockets beyond the earth's atmosphere.

The long hours and strain took their toll, however. At the end of the year, he became seriously ill. The diagnosis was that he had tuberculosis, a lung disease that often killed people. The only cure was a long rest with no activity and no excitement. He returned to his parents' home in Worcester and spent months in bed. He was discouraged and bored, but he used the time to think about the theories he had been studying for years.

He decided to apply for patents on some of his ideas at the U.S. Patent Office in Washington. Without this protection, a scientist's ideas could be stolen by someone else and used without his permission. In 1914, patents were granted to him for three of his ideas. One was for the use of a combustion chamber and nozzle for rocket fuel. Another was for a system of feeding either solid or liquid propellant fuel into the combustion chamber. The third idea was the theory of the multi-stage rocket. This was designed to overcome the problem of lifting a very heavy rocket and keeping the most important part of it in flight. It takes a huge apparatus to provide the lift required to get a giant rocket off the ground; this equipment adds a burden during the flight. Without this weight, the rocket could go much farther. Goddard figured that the best solution would be to have this extra weight dropped off after the rocket was launched. Then another, smaller rocket engine could be started to propel the rocket at higher altitudes. It could even be designed so that this one, too, would drop off once the rocket had escaped the earth's atmosphere. The air at this altitude would offer little resistance to the rocket and it wouldn't need the engine to keep its speed.

Today's space rockets use this principle. Parts of the rockets are jettisoned or dropped off at certain altitudes. This leaves the parts carrying astronauts or scientific instruments free to travel in space without the burden of the heavy part of the rocket.

When Goddard became well enough, he began teaching part-time at Clark University. Although he didn't earn much money, this gave him spare time to work on his rocket theories in the university's laboratories. Now, he felt, the time had come to do some experiments with rockets to test the ideas he had been working on for several years. The only manufactured rockets available were a kind used for signals, but these small devices were very inefficient in the way they burned their fuel. So he devised a steel chamber in the lab and fitted it with different sizes of nozzles to test the force that could be generated. For these the young inventor experimented with smokeless powder as a fuel, which hadn't been tried before. He tested a number of small rockets near Worcester, sending some of them flying across a lake at a height of 500 feet.

The public and the newspapers paid little attention to Goddard's experiments. He continued to work quietly on his projects while teaching part-time, writing his theories in scientific papers and trying to have them published whenever possible. To convince other scientists and government authorities that the rocket was feasible, he carefully gathered evidence that would prove his points. But a number of leading scientists doubted his ideas that a rocket could be propelled in outer space. They believed that the thrust of a rocket wouldn't work in space, because without the earth's atmosphere, it would have nothing to "push against."

Goddard was convinced that they were wrong. He was sure that a rocket's action under Newton's Third Law was self-contained—that it didn't need atmosphere to push against. He explained it this way: "The phenomenon is easily understood if one thinks of the ejected gas as a charge of fine shot moving with a very high velocity. The chamber will react or "kick" when this charge is fired, exactly as a shotgun "kicks" when firing a charge of ordinary shot."

To prove his point, Goddard ran a series of tests in a vacuum chamber, firing a rocket device where there was no earth's atmosphere. The rocket not only operated, but actually delivered greater thrust than it did in the atmosphere.

The next logical step in rocket development would be more elaborate tests with bigger and more powerful rockets. Goddard's immediate aim was to use the rocket to gather weather data in the earth's upper atmosphere. There was then no means of sending scientific instruments that high to record the desired data, and the rocket looked like the only possible means of doing it. Goddard proposed to send rockets from ten to twenty miles up to study air pressure, temperature and wind velocity.

But to do this he needed more money than he had. He wrote up his test results and had them printed as a book with photographs titled *A Method of Reaching Extreme Altitudes*. When the book was ready, he sent it to the Smithsonian Institution in Washington with a letter asking for a grant of money to help him do his research and build some rockets. The famous Smithsonian Institution, which was founded in 1846 for the "increase and diffusion of knowledge among men," has helped many scientists and inventors. Goddard estimated that he needed $10,000 to do his work, but he was afraid that it might seem too much to them, so he asked for $5,000. The Smithsonian promptly granted it to him.

The secretary of the Smithsonian, Dr. Charles D. Walcott, met with Goddard and encouraged him. Describing Goddard as a "lone wolf," he said, "He knew precisely what he was doing. I have never seen so much confidence."

Goddard was, indeed, a confident young scientist who knew his goal and felt he could reach it. He was a modest, quiet man who never boasted, but he never lacked self-confidence.

Soon after receiving the Smithsonian grant, World War I caused a change in his plans. Instead of working on his high-altitude research, he offered his knowledge to the Army for weapons development. The Army asked him to move to California to work on military rockets. He was soon involved in developing a type of rocket that could be fired by an infantry soldier at tanks and enemy troops. In November, 1918, Goddard demonstrated three lightweight models of this weapon, which fired a penetrating charge that could stop tanks, yet had very little "kick" for the soldier firing it. It was a resounding success, but the war ended a few days later and the Army lost all interest in rockets. Years later, this same design was the basis for the famed bazooka antitank weapon used by American soldiers in World War II.

After the war ended, Goddard returned to Clark University and resumed his rocket experiments. He continued to work toward finding the best type of rocket fuel, experimenting with dry powder, liquid oxygen and hydrogen. Each had its advantages and drawbacks, and he tried to find the best combination of fuels and combustion systems. He used his research test results in another version of his book *A Method of Reaching Extreme Altitudes,* which the Smithsonian published. It wasn't meant to attract much attention, except from his fellow scientists, but he had written something in the last part that did. He had written that it would be feasible someday to send a rocket to the moon, and he suggested that it carry a load of flash powder that would ignite when it struck the moon's surface. By hitting the dark side of the moon, the flash would be visible through powerful telescopes on earth. The newspapers seized on this as a sensational story: a scientist who wanted to go to the moon. They referred to Goddard as "the Moon Man," and suddenly the public was very interested in him.

This is not what Goddard wanted. He had simply tried to illustrate the future possibilities of rocket space travel to scientists. Wanting to get on with his quiet research, he stopped giving interviews to the hundreds of reporters who hounded him. But this just made people all the more curious about him, and newspapers began referring to him as the "Mystery Professor" and wrote of fantastic preparations he was making for his "moon journey."

The problem, as Goddard saw it, was that too many Americans were excited about this sensational aspect of his writing, but the government and other scientists weren't paying much attention to the rest of the book, which contained his serious scientific findings. In Europe, it was different. Scientists there paid a great deal of attention to his report, which was reprinted in many countries. The Germans were especially interested. Hermann Oberth, a student at a German university who would later be recognized as one of the world's great rocket scientists, wrote to Goddard for more copies of his writings. Years later, during World War II, it would be seen that the Germans learned much from Goddard's work when they built their V-2 rockets. They were very similar to Goddard's design.

Many foreign nations, including Russia, Japan, Germany and Italy, wrote to Goddard asking for his services and offering to pay him well. But he turned them all down, even though he received little support from his own government after World War I.

After 1920, Goddard was working almost entirely with liquid fuels for his rockets. Solid fuels were sufficient for short, horizontal flights, like those of the bazooka rocket weapon, but they were too unreliable for lifting larger rockets and keeping them vertical. If they were packed too tightly, they burned too slowly and the rocket wouldn't lift. If they were packed too loosely, they caused a sudden explosion, which was useless.

Goddard spent much of his time working on the plumbing system needed to pump liquid oxygen and a liquid fuel, such as gasoline, from separate tanks into the combustion chamber. Here the liquids combined and burned, which turned them to very hot gasses under high pressure. The great force of this expansion lifted the rocket. As the rockets he devised became more complicated, he had to keep changing the fuel feeding system.

By now, the "lone wolf" professor was married to Esther Kisk Goddard, a young woman who had worked for the president of Clark University. She proved to be a valuable partner, working with him on his experiments in many capacities. She became the photographer for his tests, taking still shots and motion pictures of the rocket launchings.

Their test equipment was home-built in some cases—anything they could borrow or scrape together. As a rocket-launching frame, Goddard bought a farm windmill from Sears, Roebuck and converted it to his use. When he found a chemical company that threw away liquid oxygen, he arranged to buy it cheaply by picking it up himself.

The grant from the Smithsonian had run out, and it was difficult to get much more, since the Institution's funds were low at the time. Goddard simply had to "make do" with the limited money he could get, but while this slowed the pace of his experiments, it didn't stop him from working hard with his limited equipment.

A friendly woman who owned a farm in Auburn, Massachusetts, on the outskirts of Worcester, offered to let Goddard use the farm as a site for testing his rockets. He used this site for a long series of test flights, hauling the rocket and launching equipment from the laboratory at Clark in old cars. He even used horse-drawn sleighs in winter.

A milestone was achieved in March 1926 with the flight of the world's first liquid-fueled rocket. It was a cold, clear day and snow covered the ground at the farm. When everything was ready, Mrs. Goddard got her camera. An assistant, Henry Sachs, lit the engine with a blowtorch at the end of a long pole. For a few seconds, the rocket did not lift, but there was a flame and a roar. Then the rocket rose, slowly at first, then picking up speed tremendously. It rose to four times its own height, moving at a speed of sixty miles an hour, before it began to lose altitude. Then it smashed into a muddy field about two hundred and twenty feet away. It was a short flight, but then, so was the first flight of the Wright Brothers' airplane.

More tests and more flights followed. In 1929, a more elaborate rocket was launched that contained a barometer, thermometer and a small camera to take pictures of the instrument readings in flight. The rocket rose ninety feet on this occasion, and the flight lasted eighteen and a half seconds. The camera and barometer were parachuted safely back to earth.

The noise of the rocket flight caused a great commotion among local residents, and the press picked up the story. "Terrific Explosion as Professor Goddard of Clark Shoots his Moon Rocket," was the headline in a Worcester paper. The state fire marshal warned Goddard of the danger of setting off forest fires in the area, and it appeared that many people were against further test flights at the farm.

Goddard knew that he would have to look for some other, less crowded place to conduct future tests. But this would require money, especially if it meant moving far away from his job at Clark. Luckily, his work happened to attract the attention of Col. Charles A. Lindbergh, the famous aviator who had made the first solo flight across the Atlantic. Lindbergh felt that Goddard was a pioneer much like himself, who was working against odds for a dream. He visited Goddard and talked about the possibilities of rocket flight. The visit made him so interested in Goddard's work that he went to the wealthy Guggenheim family to ask for funds for the inventor. The Guggenheim family had established the Guggenheim Fund for the Promotion of Aeronautics, and this organization made a $50,000 grant to Goddard. The Carnegie Institution also made a smaller grant for test facilities.

Now Goddard could move to a new test site in an uncrowded area. After scanning maps and weather charts, he selected New Mexico, which had many sunny days and was warm enough to conduct flights all year round. Piling into his car with Mrs. Goddard, he drove west to search for the right location in that state. He found it at the Mescalero Ranch near Roswell, a great open area with very little population. With his wife and four assistants who had worked with him at Clark, he set up shop there in

1930. He stayed until 1941, except for a break in 1932-34, conducting his lonely research projects. The world might not be paying much attention to him, but the work he was doing would be tremendously important in the future.

Goddard was happy to be able to work full-time on his rocket projects, rather than using just the time he had left after teaching. The shop he fixed up was crude, and so were the living conditions. The crew of assistants stayed in an isolated ranch house with the Goddards, and Mrs. Goddard cooked all the meals, besides helping with the experiments. One of her jobs was to put out the small grass fires that the rockets always started when they were launched. But the experiments went well, and Goddard made good progress in improving fuels and mechanical systems for the rockets.

In a letter to a friend in 1937 he wrote, "It is, as you can imagine, a fascinating life. The drawback is that until there has been a great and spectacular height reached, no layman, and not many scientists, will concede that you have accomplished anything, and of course there is a vast amount of spade work, of much importance, that must be done first."

In 1940, Goddard met with a joint committee of Army and Navy officials and presented information on both solid- and liquid-fueled rockets. He asked if they would be interested in developing rockets for military use, using his advanced knowledge, but they turned him down. He then met with Air Corps officials and proposed the use of rockets

Robert H. Goddard, conducting one of his early experiments with a solid-fuel steel combustion chamber at Clark University, Worcester, Massachusetts, in 1915. (Photo courtesy of Smithsonian Institution)

Robert Goddard, displaying one of his early rockets ready for launching in 1928. The rocket's length was less than fifteen feet, but it was a successful ancestor of today's space missiles. (Photo courtesy of Smithsonian Institution)

Robert Goddard, second from left, posing with his assistants and the wreckage of a rocket after a flight at Auburn, Massachusetts in 1929. This rocket was the first to carry a camera, thermometer and barometer on a flight. (Photo courtesy of Smithsonian Institution)

In the early 1930s, Robert Goddard was already experimenting with an apparatus for solar energy in rockets. Today, solar energy is a standard power source for space satellite equipment. (Photo courtesy of Smithsonian Institution)

In 1935, Robert Goddard was hard at work on larger, more advanced rockets in his workshop at Roswell, New Mexico. The remote desert location was perfect for conducting experimental flights. (Photo courtesy of Smithsonian Institution)

Robert Goddard, making adjustments on one of his rocket combustion chambers in 1940. Lacking large-scale financial backing, Goddard made many of his own rocket parts with the help of a small staff. (Photo courtesy of Smithsonian Institution)

for jet-assisted takeoffs of bomber aircraft. They expressed little interest. (Several years later, military planes used jet-assisted takeoff equipment on a large scale.)

Meanwhile, the German Army had had a rocket-testing station in operation since 1932, using many full-time rocket experts and government money. Using basic knowledge they gained from Goddard's published writing, they were on their way to building their wartime V-2 rockets.

At times, Goddard's funds ran so low that he had to give up his New Mexico tests during the 1930s, but he resumed them as soon as he could find another grant. He continued working on more flights, keeping the pressure constant, avoiding explosions of the combustion chambers by using different types of cooling systems, studying stronger, lighter materials, and making gyroscopes and other equipment for guiding the rocket's flight.

Rockets were often unpredictable in flight; they might swerve from their path and twist into another direction. To correct this, Goddard invented a control mechanism consisting of an elaborate gyroscope to control the guiding vanes on the rocket. These vanes were designed to keep the rocket flying straight by acting like a boat's rudder. A rudder works against the stream of water behind a boat, as a means of steering the boat. The vanes would work the same way, turning in the stream of gas coming from the rocket engine's nozzle. The gyroscope was also designed to release a parachute just before the rocket reached its greatest height. The parachute would let the rocket float back to earth safely and avoid smashing into the ground. This important invention, along with many others, made possible the later improvements in rocket technology that we see today.

The rockets continued to get bigger and to fly higher and for longer distances. Moving at supersonic speed, an eighty-five-pound rocket flew nearly a mile and a half. As the performances improved, Goddard continued to search for refinements. He decided that he needed a less-complicated fuel-feed system that would be more dependable than those he had been using. He thought of turbine-driven pumps for the fuel and soon went to work to devise a lightweight pump-turbine unit that could give tremendous thrust. It was important to keep the weight down for long-range flights.

In earlier rockets, liquid oxygen and gasoline had been forced into the combustion chamber by nitrogen escaping from a tank in the rocket. If you could eliminate this tank, it would reduce the rocket's weight. So he designed a centrifugal pump system that could be self-sustaining after it started pumping. It required a pump between the gasoline tank and the chamber and another one between the oxygen tank and the chamber.

The challenge was to find a way to start the pumps and to keep them going. He decided that the solution was a turbine drive. The turbine blades were mounted on a shaft inside the rocket. They would be started by the high-speed flow of nitrogen from a tank outside the rocket while it was on the ground. Once started, the turbine blades would turn, along with the shaft, and this would make the pumps work.

To keep the blades turning, Goddard devised a pipe connection to capture some of the hot gasses that normally would rush out the nozzle of the rocket engine. This heat would be vaporized, and under pressure, this vapor would turn the blades and keep the pumps operating.

Existing centrifugal pumps were too heavy for this purpose, so Goddard and his crew worked on lighter ones. In 1940, they finally succeeded in making miniature pumps so small they could be held in a person's hand. Tests proved these pumps could drive rockets that weighed nearly five hundred pounds.

As Goddard brought his liquid-fueled rockets to a high degree of development, he tried, in one form or another, just about all of the ideas that have since been developed in rockets and guided missiles, including gyroscope controls, clustered engines, research instruments, turbine-driven pumps, gimbal-mounted tail sections for steering, automatic firing and releasing devices, and many others. Another idea he had as far back as his student days was to use solar energy to operate rocket motors. Today, every satellite uses solar energy.

Goddard reached the high point, in more ways than one, of his work in New Mexico when one of his rockets flew some 9,000 feet high over the desert country. But his work was interrupted once again by war. After the start of World War II, the Navy asked him to come east and work at its Bureau of Aeronautics, as Director of Research on Jet Propulsion. He closed up the little shop in New Mexico "for the duration of the war," he said. He planned to go back there later and continue his high-altitude rocket research. It was hard to leave his work, which had gone so well, but winning the war had to be the most important thing for him now.

One of his main assignments for the Navy was developing a system of jet-assisted takeoff for bombers and seaplanes. Ironically, this was the same system he had proposed before the war, which military officials had then rejected. He brought his group of workers with him to Annapolis, Maryland, where they worked until the war was nearly over in 1945. The jet-assisted-takeoff project was successful, and the device was flight tested many times to perfect it.

Another project was developing a rocket motor with variable thrust, which could be controlled by a pilot. The military wanted a rocket motor on an airplane that was as dependable as a water faucet, so that a pilot could speed it up or slow it down, the way you turn a faucet on or off. This was a very tricky challenge because of the explosive nature of the fuel. A slight miscalculation could mean a leak of gas or liquid oxygen, and there would be an explosion.

Goddard worked long hours on this project, month after month, and he succeeded with it after hundreds of proving-stand tests. The task had seemed nearly impossible, but in the end the rocket airplane engine worked as dependably as the military officials had hoped. The engine could idle for fifteen seconds before takeoff, then quickly speed up to the three-hundred-pound pressure necessary to get the power needed for takeoff. It could then be idled again for leveling off, and then raced up to five hundred pounds of thrust for flight. The pilot could make the plane do anything he would need it to do in combat. Later, this same engine design was used in America's high-altitude, pre-space mission flights, in such aircraft as the X-2 and the X-15. These planes easily passed the speed of sound.

The final project that Goddard worked on at Annapolis was a small liquid-oxygen gasoline rocket. This pressure-fed rocket was designed to be adapted to a guided missile in the future.

The long, exhausting work hours were affecting his health. He developed a constant cough, which he believed might indicate a return of his old tuberculosis problem. He kept on working, but it became hard for him to talk after a while. When he finally entered a hospital for an operation, doctors found that he had cancer of the throat. A few weeks later, in August 1945, he died. The war was ending, and in another decade or so, the United States would finally launch its great effort to conquer space with rocket engines and guided missiles. It would have to work hard to overcome the lead of the Soviet Union's space program.

Robert Goddard would have loved to contribute to the great space effort of the 1960s and 1970s. But he had, in fact, already contributed more than any other person to space flight. Dr. Wernher von Braun, the great German rocket scientist who later played a key role in the U.S. space program, described Goddard as his boyhood hero. He commented, "He was ahead of us all. In light of what has happened since his untimely death, we can only wonder what might have been if America realized earlier the implications of his work. I have not the slightest doubt that the United States today would enjoy unchallenged leadership in space exploration, had adequate support and recognition been provided to him."

It is unfortunate that the recognition Goddard deserved came after his death. In 1959, the United States government paid one million dollars to Mrs. Goddard and the Guggenheim Foundation, which had sponsored his work, for government use of more than two hundred of his patents. At Wernher von Braun's urging, the American Rocket Society erected a marker commemorating his launching in 1926 of the world's first liquid-fueled rocket. The United States Congress voted to award Goddard the rare honor of the Congressional Medal in 1959. The Smithsonian Institution, which had supported his work over a number of years, awarded him the famous Langley Medal, which had been given to only eight men before him.

The National Aeronautics and Space Administration named one of its major facilities, the Goddard Space Flight Center, after him in 1959. The American Rocket Society and other organizations give awards in Goddard's name. At the Air Force Academy, students compete for the Goddard Award, which is presented each year to the student with the highest grades in mathematics. The Guggenheim Foundation has also honored him by creating the Robert Hutchings Goddard Professorships at Princeton University and the California Institute of Technology. These programs sponsor science professors who teach at these schools.

There are many fascinating Goddard exhibits to be seen in various places. They contain rockets he worked on, mechanisms he invented, photos of his experiments and diagrams of his ideas. The National Air and Space Museum of the Smithsonian Institution in Washington displays some of these items. Clark University and Worcester Polytechnic Institute, where he attended school, also have exhibits of his work. The Roswell Museum in Roswell, New Mexico, near the site where he worked so many years, has a fine exhibit.

In 1979, Goddard was inducted into the National Inventors Hall of Fame at Arlington, Virginia. The Hall of Fame, which is administered by the National Inventors Hall of Fame Foundation, chooses only those inventors who make major and lasting contributions to the nation's welfare. The

Selection Committee of the Foundation chose Robert Goddard specifically for his invention of a Control Mechanism for Rocket Apparatus, which is covered by U.S. Patent No. 2,397,657.

In his application for this patent, Goddard wrote: "This invention relates to rockets and rocket craft which are propelled by combustion apparatus using liquid fuel and a liquid to support combustion, such as liquid oxygen. Such combustion apparatus is disclosed in my prior application Serial No. 327,257, filed April 1, 1940.

"It is the general object of my present invention to provide control mechanism by which the necessary operative steps and adjustments for such mechanism will be effected automatically and in predetermined and orderly sequence.

"To the attainment of this objective, I provide control mechanism which will automatically initiate and sustain flight and which will automatically discontinue flight in a safe and orderly manner."

Today, there is a high degree of automation in space flights. Without these automatic mechanisms, the complicated equipment could not work and we would have no space flights. The ideas for today's space vehicles came from Robert Goddard's early inventions such as his Control Mechanism for Rocket Apparatus. If space scientists and engineers had not been able to use Goddard's proven ideas as a starting point, our space program might be years behind the point where it is now. We might be still working toward putting a man on the moon. Many of the great scientific achievements of our nation and our aerospace industry might not have been made if it were not for Goddard.

Goddard is not recognized just for one patented invention, of course. His great stream of ideas and inventions resulted in 214 patents granted to him during his career.

Robert Goddard would not be surprised at the wonderful progress our nation has made in space. He knew his ideas were contributing toward this goal and he knew that we would have space flights, in spite of those who doubted him. He said in 1904, "It is difficult to say what is impossible, for the dream of yesterday is the hope of today and the reality of tomorrow."

CHARLES GOODYEAR

---

*The Invincible
Rubber Man*

OF ALL the qualities an inventor needs—curiosity, respect for scientific principles, flexible thinking and faith—*persistence* might be the most important. Certainly this was true of Charles Goodyear, the man who invented a process called *vulcanization*, which made it possible to make thousands of useful products out of rubber.

After trying for years and finally succeeding with his important discovery, Charles Goodyear spent more years trying to convince people that it really *was* a useful invention. In the meantime, he and his family lived in poverty, barely managing to get enough food to eat. Goodyear was thrown into debtors prison many times because he didn't have enough money to pay his bills. Friends and relatives urged him to give up his rubber experiments and find a better way to make a living, but he refused to abandon his dream. He persisted in going on with his efforts to make rubber a useful material, and by the end of his life, he knew that he had succeeded.

Virtually all the rubber products we use today—automobile tires, pencil erasers, boots, shoe soles, inflatable rafts, rainwear and thousands of others—owe their existence to the discovery of vulcanization by this stubborn, resourceful inventor.

Born in New Haven, Connecticut, in 1800, Charles Goodyear was influenced in early childhood by his father's interest in inventing things. He watched while his father experimented with new types of pitchforks and scythes for farmers as well as spoons, clocks and pearl buttons. When Charles was five, his father established a manufacturing plant at Naugatuck, near New Haven. The first pearl buttons in America were made in this plant, as were most of the metal buttons on the uniforms of American soldiers in the War of 1812.

His father held patents on a number of his inventions. Probably the most important was for his spring steel pitchfork. At this time, farmers generally used heavy, wrought-iron pitchforks made for them by local blacksmiths. These tools became battered and bent very quickly. The Goodyear pitchfork was not only lighter, but the steel prongs did not become bent as easily.

Charles was the first child in the family, but he soon had plenty of playmates. Four brothers and a sister were born after him. As the oldest of the children, Charles was expected to help his father at work when he wasn't in school. He didn't mind, because he was interested in his father's inventions and manufacturing. He was a fairly serious, sensible boy who liked to read and to tinker with mechanical things to see how they worked.

Charles also became interested in religion and considered becoming a minister. But his father needed him to help in the family business, so he abandoned the idea of a career in religion. When he finished high school at seventeen, his father arranged for him to be an apprentice at a hardware company in Philadelphia for four years. This was a common practice in the early 1800s. Instead of going to college, a young person often served an apprenticeship, learning a business or a skill while working for a company. When finished with the apprenticeship, the young person was considered experienced in the type of work he had learned and could go out into the world, seeking jobs.

When Charles had completed his on-the-job learning of the hardware business, he returned to Connecticut to go into business with his father. Their company, called A. Goodyear and Son, became quite prosperous, manufacturing and selling pitchforks and other hardware items.

Charles, now fully grown, was a thin, short man of frail health. As a child, he had suffered from dyspepsia, a stomach condition that makes it difficult to digest food, and this disease was to trouble him the rest of his life. Nevertheless, he seemed to be enjoying life as the young partner of a prosperous business. In 1824, he married Clarissa Beecher, the daughter of a Naugatuck innkeeper. The young couple had a daughter, Ellen, born in 1825, and they were able to live very comfortably on the income Charles made from the family business.

Having learned the hardware selling business in Philadelphia, Charles thought it would be a good idea for him to move to that city and open a retail store, selling the goods made by A. Goodyear and Son. He and Clarissa moved there in 1826, and the new store got off to a successful start. They had a second daughter, Cynthia, in 1827.

So far, everything had gone well in their lives. Charles was working too hard, though, putting in long hours to make the business a success. In 1829, he was stricken with severe attacks of dyspepsia and had to spend a long time in bed. Even worse, the failure of his health was soon followed by the failure of the family business. Charles and his father had expanded the business too rapidly, going into debt to spread its operations to many states. They had granted credit to too many customers and when a recession hit the country, the customers were unable to pay them. In order to pay their own debts, Charles and his father gave up their ownership of the business. But this still left them with many debts to pay, and the laws of that time demanded that debtors be punished by going to prison. Charles went to prison for the first time in Philadelphia in 1830.

His daughter, Ellen, remembered that her father was missing one day and her mother explained to her that he was in jail, not because he had done something bad, but because he had too many debts to pay. Clarissa left Ellen in charge of her younger sister Cynthia and the new baby, Sarah, born in 1830, while she visited Charles every day in his cell.

Charles regarded the jail sentence as a misfortune but not a tragedy, and he tried to look on the bright side of it. He believed that he learned some valuable lessons about life in jail. He decided that a man with a good purpose in life could benefit by discovering that he could be as happy within prison walls as he could outside.

Charles used the long, idle days to tinker and think about inventions. He even invented an improvement for farm machinery and sold it while in prison, thus earning some money to support his family. He also used the time to think about what he wanted to do next in life, now that his business was dead.

Over the next several years, Charles was in and out of prison a number of times for debts, but he kept struggling to earn a meager income by inventing things. He was awarded two patents in 1831, for a "safety-eye button" and for an improved spring steel pitchfork. Two more patents followed in 1832, for a new type of water faucet and a new spoon. Goodyear was obviously a genius at inventing things in a wide variety of fields. His problem was that none of these inventions were of a type that could make him rich, or even provide him with a good income.

Tragedy struck the young Goodyear family in the 1830s. At this time, before medical science was very far advanced, diseases killed many young children. This was the case with the Goodyears. A baby girl was born to them in 1831, but she died after only a few months. In 1833, their three-year-old daughter, Sarah, died. However, their first son, Charles Jr., was born that year. Mrs. Goodyear bore the weight of these tragedies valiantly while struggling with poverty and trying to encourage her husband with his inventions. He at least could take his mind off the family tragedies while working with his experiments. He continued inventing and was awarded patents on another type of faucet and an air pump in 1834 and 1835.

It was during this time that Goodyear came upon the rubber business, which would dominate the rest of his life. While visiting New York, he stopped in a store operated by the Roxbury India Rubber Company, of Roxbury, Massachusetts. Looking at a rubber inflatable life preserver for sale, he got an idea for a better inflation valve for it. He rushed home to Philadelphia, invented one, and sold it to the company. He returned to New York with other ideas and got into a long discussion with the Roxbury people about rubber.

The people of South and Central America had known and used rubber in limited ways for centuries before the early European explorers met them. Christopher Columbus and others are said to have brought samples of rubber back to Europe with them, but people in Europe didn't find much use for the material. Rubber is a sort of gum that comes from the milky sap of certain trees and shrubs. Spanish soldiers noticed that Indians made balls from it that would bounce easily into the air. They also used it to spread on clothing, to make it waterproof. The Spanish copied this idea, but it wasn't very practical because the latex coating got sticky on hot days. The name given to this substance was *caoutchouc,* but in English it came to be called rubber, because small chunks of it were used to rub marks off things, just as an eraser does today.

By the 1830s, a rubber industry had grown in England and other European countries. Factories made rubber-coated raincoats, hats, boots and fire hoses, while inventors such as Thomas Hancock experimented with more ways to use rubber. The problems with natural rubber were that it became very sticky, like glue, in hot weather and very hard and unbending in cold weather. It also had a terrible smell when it was warm.

A rubber industry also sprang up in the United States, shortly after the British industry was established. But the summers are hotter and the winters are colder in the United States than in Great Britain, and the public soon got disgusted with rubber products. The folds of raincoats would stick together in hot weather, and the smell was offensive. Thousands of pairs of rubber shoes were sold, and the owners found them hard as rock in winter and difficult to walk in.

By the time Charles Goodyear met the people from the Roxbury India Rubber Company, the industry was in trouble. Few people wanted to buy their products, and the Roxbury company was going bankrupt. They had thousands of surplus coats, hats, shoes and wagon covers they couldn't sell. The odor from this huge supply of goods was so bad that they had to bury the entire supply underground.

Goodyear had been fascinated with bits of rubber he had played with as a child, and now he became even more fascinated as he listened to the troubles of the rubber industry. "Rubber is such a wonderful substance," he said. "If only a way could be found to keep it from melting in the summer and getting brittle in the winter, it could be useful to mankind in a thousand ways."

Goodyear decided that he had found his mission in life—to discover a way to make rubber more useful. He knew that manufacturers and chemists had experimented with ways to make rubber more manageable and less sticky, and that they had failed. He didn't know anything about the substance, and he didn't have a scientific education, but he was determined to try until he found the answer, no matter how long it took him.

Back in Philadelphia, Goodyear set to work in the kitchen of his family's rented cottage. This had to serve as his "laboratory" since he had no money to hire a place. In fact, his work was interrupted several times when he had to go to jail for periods of time because he couldn't pay his debts.

In the United States, rubber was dissolved in turpentine to get it into a form that could be handled. Goodyear followed this technique, cutting his "gum" rubber into small pieces, mixing them with the turpentine and kneading them into a dough. Then he would add other materials, to see if they would affect the nature of the rubber. He would spread the mixture out on a marble slab with his wife's rolling pin.

He soon found out for himself how difficult it was going to be to find the right answer. "The substance had baffled all the efforts of chemists and manufacturers to divest it of its objectionable qualities," he noted. But this didn't discourage him in the least. Other people might have been discouraged in his position—constantly being arrested for nonpayment of debts, being sick, seeing his family live in poverty—but he kept on. He was convinced that persistence would make it possible to find the answer, even though scientific research had failed.

He wasn't close to discovering the secret of vulcanization at this time, but he did have some minor success in reducing the stickiness of rubber. He found that by mixing magnesia powder with rubber, it turned the mixture into a hard, dry, white material. He had a book cover made from this material, but it soon became soft and sticky. Next he tried making thin sheets of rubber and coating fabrics with rubber. He was elated with these results, and he convinced himself that this was enough of an advancement that he could begin manufacturing goods from the material.

Other people weren't as optimistic as he was,

but he finally convinced a friend to lend him enough money to start manufacturing rubber shoes. He moved to New Haven and started a small factory, with himself and his wife and daughters supplying most of the labor. After making up several hundred pairs of shoes, Goodyear stored them to test their quality before selling them to the public. But when summer came, the shoes melted into a mass of gum. The experiment in manufacturing had been a total failure, and his friend refused him further aid. The merchants who had supplied the factory cut off his credit, and he had to go out of business. To pay his bills, Goodyear had to sell the family's furniture. After finding a place for his family to board temporarily, he went to New York City to continue his experiments.

Other people had followed the same route as Goodyear in the 1830s: becoming rubber manufacturers and then going broke. The other business owners gave up the rubber business, but not Goodyear. He felt his try at manufacturing had been useful. It had shown him that the mixtures he had tried were not the right ones, and he could eliminate these from his future experiments.

Fortunately, he had some friends in New York City who helped him to continue his experiments. One allowed him to sleep in a room at his house and another, who was a druggist, gave him the chemicals he needed for his tests. He also got permission to use part of a small factory for his experiments. He walked three miles to it every day, carrying a jug of lime to mix with his materials. The lime seemed to make the rubber smoother, and again he felt he had found an improvement. He obtained a patent for this discovery, and he won his first awards from the Mechanics Institute of New York and the American Institute of New York, "for a new discovery in India Rubber," as it was called in 1835.

To experiment, and to advertise the uses of rubber, Goodyear made a number of clothing items out of rubber and wore them. Explaining this, he wrote, "If you meet a man who has on an India rubber cap, stock, coat, vest, and shoes, with an India rubber money purse without a cent of money in it, that is I." He also wrote that this helped his experiments, adding, "The wearing of gum elastic about the person was one of the severest tests to which it could be put."

One day, Goodyear met one of his former teachers from his school days in Connecticut while walking the streets of New York City. The teacher was shocked at the inventor's appearance. His clothing looked shabby, and he looked tired and worn. Goodyear invited him to his room, which was a tiny hole so filled with chemicals, kettles and rubber gum that there was hardly room for both of them to sit down. Explaining his experiments, he told his former teacher, "Here is something that will pay all my debts and make us comfortable." But the rubber industry had gone broke and was dead, said his visitor. "And I am the man to bring it back again," replied Goodyear.

Eventually his lime experiments proved to him that the lime had too powerful an effect on the rubber and wouldn't work. While he was thinking about what to try next, he decided to remove some bronze decoration he had painted on some rubber-coated fabric. He used nitric acid to dissolve the bronze paint, but the acid discolored the fabric, and he threw it in a trash can. A few days later, he decided that he hadn't examined the changed appearance of the rubber enough, so he took it back out of the trash can. He noticed that the rubber surface had lost its stickiness.

Goodyear followed up on this clue and developed an "acid gas" process for treating rubber. He obtained a patent on this in 1837 and tried to interest businessmen in investing in it. But he couldn't find anyone who was interested. He decided to move back to New Haven to be with his family and continue working on the acid process. Renting a small cottage there, he worked long days trying to improve his process.

His enthusiasm nearly killed him one day. Trying a secret experiment, he was working in a closed room making up solutions of metallic salts. He didn't notice that this generated large quantities of gas, which nearly suffocated him. When he was finally hauled out of the room, unconscious, he had to be placed under a doctor's care for six weeks.

Tragedy again struck the Goodyear family when their three-year-old son William died. The little cottage at New Haven was no longer a cheerful place to live, so the family packed up and moved back to New York City. A businessman whom Goodyear had met at the Mechanics Institute became interested in his acid process and agreed to help the inventor financially. They soon rented a factory building that had steam power and began producing rubberized cloth life preservers, hats, aprons and a few shoes. The products sold so well that a larger factory was rented on Staten Island in New York and a sales-room was opened in Manhattan.

Goodyear tried everything he could think of to publicize his rubber products and tell people about them. He even had his business cards made of pure rubber. He had paintings and words printed on rubber sheets and sent them to the President of the United States, who thanked him in a polite note.

Just when it seemed that Goodyear could at last be prosperous, the country suffered a severe business recession. Industries closed, people lost their jobs and stopped buying as many goods. His friend and financial backer went bankrupt. There was no more money with which to run the factory, so it closed.

Once again reduced to poverty, Goodyear and his family moved into a small cottage on the grounds of the closed factory. They didn't have to pay any rent, but they were desperately short of money for food. Goodyear made a few rubberized piano and table covers and some aprons to sell, but sales were slow and he made little money. One by one, he sold the family's furniture pieces to buy food. In order to have some furnishings in the empty house, he invited his younger brother, Robert, and his wife to move in with their furniture. While Charles Goodyear assumed the support of the combined family, Robert supplied much of the food by catching fish in the nearby bay.

Goodyear knew he hadn't found the perfect answer to the problems of making rubber useful, but his acid process did reduce the stickiness in rubber a great deal. He tried hard to convince businessmen that by using his process, they could prosper in the rubber business. But he had been talking so long and so loudly over the years about the advantages of rubber that most people didn't want to have anything to do with his "scatterbrained" ideas. They considered him slightly insane with his one, all-consuming interest.

Although most of the rubber manufacturers had gone bankrupt, the Roxbury India Rubber Company had somehow managed to stay in business, even though by 1837 it wasn't selling many goods. One day Goodyear met John Haskins, one of the principal stockholders of the firm. Haskins was impressed by some samples of rubber products Goodyear had made, and he encouraged the inventor to give up his Staten Island place and move to Roxbury, Massachusetts. Since the Roxbury factory was idle, he would be able to use part of it to continue developing his acid process.

Goodyear leaped at this opportunity. Managing to get a small loan, he moved his family to Roxbury. In a rented portion of the factory, he began producing rubberized piano and table covers and maps of sheet rubber cured by the acid process. He also invented a new method for construction of rubber shoes and obtained a patent for it in 1838. He sold the shoe patent and a license for using the acid process to a shoe company, and this brought in some much-needed money. The family was living comfortably again, a far cry from the conditions they had endured earlier.

But a dispute broke out between Goodyear and the agent for the Roxbury company, and the inventor was forced to leave the factory. The agent thought Goodyear was too impractical a man, always dreaming about great things for the future but not tending enough to business. The agent predicted that "Mr. Goodyear would get tired of building castles in the air after a while."

This latest setback hardly slowed Goodyear down, though. He met the president of a shoe company located in Woburn, Massachusetts, which had ceased to manufacture shoes and had an idle plant. Through this man, the inventor met Nathaniel Hayward, who had taken over the empty factory and who had been experimenting with rubber mixtures for some time. Hayward had tried using sulfur as an ingredient, and it seemed to dry the sticky rubber much as Goodyear's acid process did. With a common goal, the two men quickly agreed to a working arrangement. Hayward would work for Goodyear for one year and turn over the use of the Woburn factory to him.

Goodyear urged Hayward to obtain a patent for his sulfur process. When he took over the factory in 1838, he directed that much larger amounts of sulfur be added to each batch of rubber being mixed. Hayward cautioned him that he might be using too much, but Goodyear obtained improved results in his experiments with the sulfur. By combining the sulfur and acid processes, he was able to make his rubber samples even less sticky than they had been before. Goodyear helped Hayward obtain the patent for the sulfur process and then arranged to buy it from him.

The two men produced life preservers, beds, cushions, coats, capes, maps, prints and carriage cloths from rubber at the factory. When the public seemed to like the improved rubber goods, they applied to the U.S. Government for a contract to produce goods for federal use. Their big break came when they obtained a contract to produce one hundred and fifty waterproof mail bags for the government. Goodyear lost no time in notifying the newspapers about this and he received extensive publicity about the contract. Soon, just about everyone knew that Charles Goodyear was going to produce mail bags for the U.S. Government.

Unfortunately, not long afterward, everyone also knew that Charles Goodyear's mail bags turned out to be deficient. The bags had looked fine when they were finished at the factory. They were smooth, waterproof and seemed to hold their shape well. Goodyear had the bags hung by their handles as a test while he went out of town for a few weeks. When he returned, however, the bags had stretched out of shape and gotten soft and sticky. It was a failure; they could not be used by the government.

Goodyear had believed that the acid process changed the character of the rubber throughout, but in reality, it only affected the surface of the rubber. This surface treatment wasn't enough to prevent the bags from sagging from their own weight. Unfortunately, the same fate befell thousands of life preservers that he had sold around the country. They were returned for refunds and resulted in a total loss for Goodyear.

The bad publicity about the mail bags and life preservers only made the public distrust goods made of rubber even more. It also meant that Goodyear would not be able to sell his products in large enough quantities to make any money. To settle all the refunds he owed, he paid out every cent he had until he was once again penniless. Once again he sold all the family's possessions to settle his accounts, and the family turned to making shoes by hand to earn a meager living.

Not only was Goodyear faced with poverty again, but he knew that he couldn't look to his friends for sympathy any more. They advised him to give up his dream of the perfect rubber and to enter some sensible business such as hardware. They told him that if he persisted in his foolish enthusiasm for rubber, he would deserve all the bad fortune that would come his way. He had tried again and again, and there was no way to make rubber have the qualities he wanted, they said.

Goodyear had only two choices. He could take up what other people called a "respectable" occupation and live in comfort, or he could go on chasing his impossible dream and suffer for it. He was so discouraged at this point that everyone believed he would turn to a better way to make a living. But he really couldn't, any more than other great inventors could abandon their quests when they had deep inner convictions. His faith in his abilities drove him on; he borrowed a few dollars here and a few there and continued with his experiments in his home.

And then, in January 1839, came the successful discovery he had sought for so many years! Still experimenting with sulfur and other compounds, he decided to see what effect heat had on the same material that had decomposed in the mail bags. While doing this, he accidentally dropped a piece of the rubber compound on a kitchen stove. When he retrieved it, he found that it had charred like leather, rather than melting as rubber usually did. It was not sticky, and it had the qualities rubber needed to be handled.

"Look at this!" he cried to his brother, Nelson, and several friends. They could see that the inventor was excited, but they had seen him that way before. His observation meant little to them. But Goodyear was astounded at the result, and he knew he had found something very important. The next question was: How would this heat-treated piece of rubber behave in cold weather? Would it become hard and brittle as rubber always did, or would it react differently? Grabbing a nail and hammer, he rushed outside into the cold winter air and nailed the rubber to the wall.

His daughter, Ellen, later recalled the event: "As I was passing in and out of the room, I casually observed the little piece of gum that he was holding near the fire, and I noticed that he was unusually animated by some discovery he had made. He nailed the piece of gum outside the kitchen door in the intense cold. In the morning, he brought it in, holding it up exultingly. He had found it *perfectly flexible,* as it was when he put it out."

At last, the secret had been found! The combination of rubber, sulfur and *heat* eliminated the problems rubber had always had. Hot and cold weather would no longer make rubber sticky and soft, or hard as rock. This process later came to be known as vulcanization, after the name of Vulcan, the Roman god of fire.

Having made such a great discovery, Goodyear should have expected fame and fortune to follow swiftly. But it didn't happen that way. Instead, the discovery was the beginning of five of the most bitter years of his career. The inventor knew beyond a doubt that he had at last solved the rubber problem, but nobody else believed it. And try as he might, he could not convince anyone that a valuable discovery had been made. It is easy to understand why people were not enthusiastic about a new claim for rubber. Millions of dollars had been lost by the rubber manufacturing industry in the past few years, and the public was tired of false claims that rubber products were "perfect for any weather." Goodyear himself had made so many claims for improvements over the years that investors didn't trust him any more. Here he was, poverty-stricken after years of trying mightily to solve the mystery of rubber. It didn't seem to be a good risk to invest more money in his schemes. As one rubber merchant wrote, "It was about death to a man's credit to be engaged in the India rubber business."

Still, Goodyear persisted—alone. He knew that heat and sulfur together could miraculously change rubber. But how much heat? And for how long? The only way to find out was to test, over and over again. He didn't have the right machinery and heat sources to do this, and this is why he needed money for his experiments. Since he couldn't get the money or the equipment, he had to "make do" with whatever sources of heat he could find.

The winter after Goodyear's great discovery was probably the lowest period of his life. In addition to his dyspepsia problems, he experienced painful attacks of gout. He hobbled about on crutches as he conducted his experiments. It was easy enough to heat small samples of rubber over a stove, but he knew that he had to prove that large pieces of rubber could also be treated successfully in the same way. He had to do this before he could claim that vulcanization would work for all uses of rubber. When he tried heating larger pieces over an open fire, the rubber blistered before it could be heated through.

What Goodyear needed was a method of producing high heat that was uniform and easily controlled. An open fire heated some parts of the rubber more than others because the heat was not even. Lacking a uniform heat source, he had to resort to all sorts of means. With endless patience, he roasted pieces of rubber in hot sand, toasted them like marshmallows, pressed them between hot irons and steamed them over the kitchen teakettle. Whenever his patient wife took her bread from the oven, he made use of the oven's heat by putting in some foul-smelling bits of rubber.

Like a true scientist, he tried every method possible, leaving out no means that might tell him something. He kept changing his rubber mixtures and heating them for different periods—one hour, six hours, twenty-four hours. He must have been a real nuisance in his wife's kitchen, but she supported his efforts as she always had, never complaining.

At night Goodyear lay awake, wondering if the world would ever believe that he had found the secret of making rubber usable. He pawned his watch and then the household furniture and dishes. To replace the dishware, he made rubber plates and bowls for the family to use.

Because his kitchen experiments did not tell him what he wanted to know, he made the rounds

Charles Goodyear, the "Invincible Rubber Man." After trying for years to discover the secret of vulcanization he succeeded, but he had to spend more years convincing people that he had a useful invention. He suffered poverty and hardship for much of his life. (Photo courtesy of Smithsonian Institution)

This drawing shows Charles Goodyear experimenting
with rubber compounds in the kitchen of his rented
home. Rubber was of little practical use until Goodyear
found a way to keep it from getting sticky in hot weather
and brittle in the winter. (Photo courtesy of The
Goodyear Tire and Rubber Company)

Charles Goodyear's invention of vulcanization made possible the giant rubber industry of today. Here, a mixture of rubber and chemicals is blended into a compound that will become the tread of a radial tire. More than a million tons of rubber are used in automobile tires every year.

Unvulcanized radial tires are inspected before going into a curing press to be molded into shape. Without the "curing" or vulcanization, the tires would become hard as rock in winter and sticky as chewing gum in summer.

The unvulcanized tires on the left and right will be "cooked" for fifteen minutes in the presses behind them. The presses vulcanize the rubber and mold the tires in the correct shape. This universal process stems directly from the "cooking" experiments conducted by Charles Goodyear over many years. (Photos courtesy of The Goodyear Tire and Rubber Company)

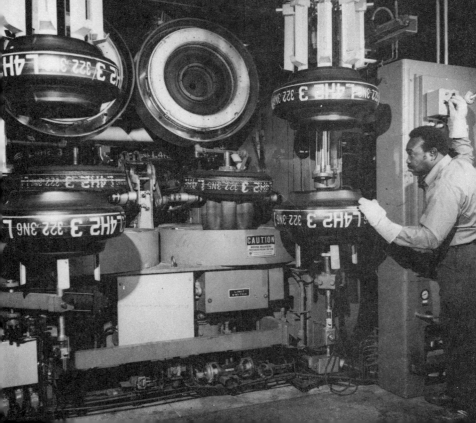

of the factories and shops in Woburn, asking to use their heat sources. He would seek to use an oven after working hours or to hang a piece of rubber in a coal boiler.

A fireman in one factory boiler room recalled: "He used to be fussing about with these samples, and I thought it was silly and boy's play-like, and I used to laugh at it. I used to be sorry for him, for I thought he was spending money to no use, and I thought the man could not afford it."

The village blacksmith and the factory workers considered Goodyear as a sort of harmless lunatic and a bit of a nuisance, but they let him use their furnaces whenever they could.

As the winter wore on, life became harder for the Goodyear family. It was becoming increasingly difficult to get enough money for food, and Charles needed money for more rubber samples. They managed to survive only through the charity of neighbors, who gave them milk and food.

One neighbor wrote later, "Their family was sick, and I was called to be with them. I found they had not fuel to burn, nor food to eat, and did not know where to get a morsel of food from one day to another, except it was sent in to them." This woman added that the poverty was caused by Goodyear's "experimenting so much on the rubber, and spending all the money he could get on that business, until he was entirely destitute."

As badly as the inventor felt about his family's living conditions, he was convinced that above all else he must continue to perfect his discovery. He said it would be better to beg for charity if necessary than to have his discovery lost to the world.

Goodyear felt that his big break might come if he could get enough money to take some of his samples to New York City and find some business investors. An acquaintance told him that if he would come to Boston, he would lend him fifty dollars to make the trip. Hobbling on pain-wracked feet through the snow, Goodyear walked the eight miles from Woburn to Boston and took a hotel room. The next day, to his horror, the acquaintance refused to give him the loan. Since Goodyear had no money to pay his hotel bill, he was thrown out. Filled with shame and crushed with disappointment, he wandered aimlessly through the snow-filled streets of Boston late into the night. The next day, he walked the eight miles back to his home. He was greeted with the news that his two-year-old son was dying. The boy had been in good health when he had left home a few days before, but had caught a fever.

The child died a few days later. Unable to pay for a funeral, Goodyear hauled the little body to the graveyard in a borrowed wagon while the rest of the family walked behind.

The next year, the inventor finally managed to go to New York City. Some merchants were impressed with what he had to show them, and they provided him with enough funds to support his family while he experimented in a small way. The experiments were all devoted to new methods of heating. At Woburn, an iron box was made and set into a small brick furnace. Strips of rubberized cloth were formed into an endless belt, which was heated as it passed over a roller in the bottom of the box and another at the end. Not long afterward, Goodyear hired a factory at Springfield, Massachusetts, and built another, larger heater of brick.

The job of perfecting the vulcanization process was difficult. The rubber goods often blistered, sometimes partly and sometimes all the way through. If the rubber wasn't heated enough, it would come out sticky. Other times, it would burn when heated too much. Despite the long series of disappointments, Goodyear slowly learned the best methods of heating rubber. His experiments gradually taught him that his sulfur needed to be bone-dry, that the sulfur must be free of acid, that his fires and heaters had to be regulated with great skill in order to raise the heat slowly and evenly. He learned many little techniques that meant the difference between charred, melted or blistered goods and smooth, firm "cured" rubber.

Even with his limited financial backing, Goodyear once more found himself in jail in Springfield for nonpayment of debts. But he paid back all his creditors later, with money earned from selling licenses of his process to manufacturers.

One source of help at this time was the former teacher he had met earlier in New York. This man had since become a successful woolen manufacturer, and he lent the inventor considerable sums of money.

By this time, he was impressed with the results Goodyear had obtained. The inventor had found that steam under pressure, applied to the rubber for four to six hours at around 270 degrees Fahrenheit, gave him the most uniform results.

When Goodyear told his former teacher that rubber threads interwoven with cloth would produce a "puckered" effect then very fashionable in men's shirts, the man set up two factories to produce these shirts. These "shirred" goods, as they were called, proved very popular. The factories made profits, and Goodyear got a small share of the money.

Goodyear wanted to apply for patents on his 1839 discovery of vulcanization, but he wanted patents in foreign countries as well as in the United States. He didn't have enough money to make all the samples he would need for patents, and it would require trips to France and England to apply for his patents in those countries. Finally, in 1844, he was awarded a patent in the United States. He also received a patent in France, but when he applied in England, he found that the English rubber scientist, Thomas Hancock, had beaten him by a few weeks. Hancock had been trying for twenty years to find a process to cure rubber. He had seen some samples of Goodyear's vulcanized rubber and, noticing that they contained sulfur, took that clue and "reinvented" vulcanization. Goodyear considered this an unfair theft of his invention, but he was unable to do anything about it, although he tried in the English courts.

Being a dreamer and an impractical man, Goodyear was not an able businessman. He made some very bad deals, allowing manufacturers to use his process under license for ridiculously small fees. He could have become a wealthy man if he had been shrewder about business deals, but he wasn't very interested in making money. He never wavered from his life's mission to make rubber useful to all the world, and he was only interested in his experiments to perfect the use of it.

He did try to protect his patents against people who tried to steal them. A number of unscrupulous manufacturers used his vulcanization process without paying him for the right to use it, and he spent a lot of time fighting this. Against these "patent pirates" he was forced to prosecute thirty-two cases all the way to the United States Supreme Court with the help of attorneys. In one famous court case, called "The Great India Rubber Suit," his attorney was Daniel Webster, who was the U.S. Secretary of State at the time. Webster took a leave of absence from his job to represent Goodyear against a man who was trying to steal his patent. After a two-day speech, Webster won the case in court.

During the last ten years of his life, the 1850s, Goodyear lived more comfortably most of the time than he had earlier. But it was a "boom or bust" existence; there were times when he could travel in style and his family could live well. At other times, he found himself short of money again and back in jail. When he received money from manufacturers who used his process under license, he would spend it quickly on more experiments and equipment, or for trips to publicize rubber.

Although he was in poor health and compelled to walk with crutches, Goodyear went to London with his family to exhibit in a great fair, "The Exhibition of the Works of All Nations." It was held in the Crystal Palace and was much like a world's fair. Goodyear called his exhibit "Vulcanite Court," and it was given a prominent position in the main hall. Pouring every cent he had, plus some borrowed money, into it, Goodyear spent $30,000 on the exhibit. It was a magnificent exhibit, made entirely of rubber. It included a large number of rubber items, including sofas, chairs, fruit plates, card trays, brooches and rings set with jewels, fruit knives, fans, opera glasses, jewel boxes, picture frames, eye glasses, ink stands, corkscrews, pen holders, pencil cases, drinking cups, buttons, syringes, surgical instruments, canes, umbrellas, combs and brushes. Rubber balloons, inflated with hydrogen, floated over this grand display. Ranging up to six feet in diameter, they were painted in multi-colors with several representing king-size world globes. Prizes were awarded for rubber displays, and Goodyear won the highest honor possible.

Goodyear spent several years in England and some time in France during the 1850s, trying to spread the word about the wonders of rubber. While he and his family were living in England, Clarissa, his wife and mother of his nine children, died. The loss of his faithful partner in life was a terrible blow to him. As Daniel Webster said about her, "In all his distress, and in all his trials, she was willing to participate in his sufferings, and endure everything, and hope everything; she was willing to be poor; she was willing to go to prison if necessary when he went to prison; she was willing to share with him everything, and that was his only solace."

Later, the lonely inventor married twenty-year-old Fanny Wardell of London. Although he was fifty-four at the time, the difference in their ages mattered little; she was a devoted wife to him for the rest of his life.

In November 1854, Goodyear, his children and the new Mrs. Goodyear arrived in Paris to exhibit at another world's fair. This time he had an even more elaborate display. Two of the exhibits were portrait paintings of Goodyear by a famous artist, painted on hard rubber panels. This exhibit was also a huge success, and Goodyear's fame spread.

But, as usual, the inventor's careless handling of money came back to haunt him. Through a minor technicality in French law that was not due to any fault of his, his French patent was ruled invalid. He had already sold licenses to French manufacturers to use his process and borrowed money from them. Now that he was not entitled to receive payment for use of his process, he had to pay the money back. When he couldn't he was thrown into a French jail.

While he was in the jail, Emperor Napoleon III of France saw his exhibit at the fair and awarded him the Grand Medal of Honor and the Cross of the Legion of Honor, two very high awards. His son, Charles Jr., had to bring him the awards in his jail cell. He was soon released, however, and was treated with honor for the rest of his stay in France.

Goodyear spent the next couple of years in England, trying to regain his health. A son was born to him but died in infancy. Another son was born in 1858, shortly after the Goodyears returned to the United States. But this son, too, died at the age of one year.

Goodyear purchased a home in Washington, D.C., not far from the White House. Owning a home was new to him, since he had spent his life constantly moving from one rented place to another. The house was equipped with a complete laboratory and an experimental tank so that he could continue his tests and ideas. He enjoyed a peaceful existence here with the loving care of his wife. A daughter was born to them in 1860. The house was probably more expensive than he could afford, for his income from licensed manufacturers was small, because of the poor business arrangements he had made. About two dozen companies were using the Goodyear vulcanization process, but his share of their profits was tiny.

Yet this concerned him very little. He was satisfied to see his dream come true. Millions of people were using rubber products of every kind, and a great rubber industry had been established, just as he had predicted years before when no one would listen to him. He had found the key with his vulcanization that made it all possible.

Today, more than a century later, chemists still don't completely understand the molecular change that comes over rubber when it is vulcanized. They do know, as Goodyear knew, that under heat the rubber compound grows stronger, more resistant to heat and cold, yet remains flexible.

Such qualities have inspired a wide range of products that would have delighted Goodyear. He foresaw many of them—jotting one idea after another in his notebook: rubber gloves, toys, conveyor belts, watertight seals, balloons, printing rollers, rubber bands. He didn't know about the automobile, of course, or the great use for rubber that would be created by tires.

Still, he wouldn't be surprised if he visited a tire-manufacturing plant today. The formula remains the same, even though synthetic rubber made from petroleum has largely replaced natural rubber. Sulfur is still the main ingredient used for vulcanizing. The huge machinery that mangles raw rubber into a sort of dough would remind him of the long hours he spent kneading his rubber pieces with his wife's rolling pin.

He knew, too, that his place was secure in history. He would have been delighted that he was inducted into the National Inventors Hall of Fame in 1976, as one of a select group of great inventors who conceived the technological advances that this nation fosters through its patent system. He was chosen for his Patent Number 3,633 called "Improvement in India Rubber Fabrics." He probably would also be pleased that today's Goodyear Tire and Rubber Company, formed many years after his death, honored him by naming the company after him.

Charles Goodyear died in New York City on July 1, 1860, while en route to visit a daughter in Connecticut. Some people might have thought that he would have died a bitter man, having seen the profits of his invention go to others.

But he didn't. In his autobiography, which he had printed and bound in rubber, he wrote: "Life should not be estimated exclusively by the standard of dollars and cents. I am not disposed to complain that I have planted and others have gathered the fruits. A man has cause for regret only when he sows and *no one* reaps."

THOMAS A. EDISON

*The Wizard
of Menlo Park*

A PROFESSIONAL inventor today, working in advanced scientific disciplines, needs a good education in the sciences and mathematics. Corporate research teams and university research organizations, where most of today's inventions are produced, operate on an advanced level of scientific knowledge gained through long study. The general rule is: Get a good education if your goal is to be an inventor.

The most famous exception to this rule was Thomas A. Edison. With 1,093 patents to his name, he has been called "the most productive inventor in the history of the United States, and possibly the most productive in the history of the human race." With no formal education beyond the age of twelve, this grassroots genius typified the American dream of success. A plain, Midwestern farmboy starting with no money, he became wealthy and one of the most famous Americans of his time by hard work and the rare talent he possessed. "There is no substitute for hard work," he once said. "Genius is ninety-nine percent perspiration and one percent inspiration." While he may have been too modest about his genius, his career was proof that genius coupled with hard work can lead to outstanding success.

Any one of Thomas Alva Edison's major inventions—the phonograph, the motion picture, improvements in the telephone, the telegraph and the stock ticker—would have been a major career achievement by itself, but he accomplished all these and much more. His most important contribution—the one that has had the greatest impact on all our lives —was the invention of a workable incandescent light bulb. A light bulb is such a common product today that it is hard to realize the significance of its invention until one considers that it made possible the Age of Electricity. For having invented the light bulb, Edison had to design our entire electrical system to make this light available to millions of homes, offices and factories. He produced a fantastic array of related goods: dynamos to generate electric power, cables, power lines, switches, sockets, junction boxes, wires, insulators, meters, fuses, connectors, conductors, manhole boxes, methods of interior wiring, voltage regulators, bulbs and scores of other devices. He literally created an entire industry for electricity, the energy form on which modern progress is based.

Edison's inventions brought changes in people's lives that were undreamed of before that time.

From the beginning of the human race, darkness had limited human activities. The dim, flickering light of candles, oil lamps, gas lamps and fireplaces made it difficult to read or to do any other activity that required sight. It meant that work and business were restricted to daylight hours, thus limiting man's industrial production of needed goods. It was common for most people to go to bed soon after sunset, because when darkness fell, they could not do anything else.

When Edison brought electric light to the world, he lengthened mankind's day, making it possible to enjoy evening leisure activities and to conduct work and business for more hours in a day. Factories were able to operate two or more shifts to produce the goods people needed and stores could remain open evenings. Today, our lives are far more convenient and comfortable than those of our ancestors. With his electricity system, Edison made possible many of the things we take for granted: radio and television, electric tools, loudspeakers, toasters, tape recorders, electric shavers and toothbrushes, electric typewriters, thermostats, traffic lights, elevators, computers, refrigerators, washers and dryers, electric power for factories, offices and stores, night baseball and football games and much more.

Thomas Alva Edison was born in the small town of Milan, Ohio, in 1847, the youngest of seven children. His father wasn't a very successful man; he tried a number of businesses and jobs and was usually in financial difficulties. Thomas, whose nickname was "Al," for Alva, was a high-spirited boy who loved to play pranks. He was a difficult child to raise because he had his own stubborn ideas about everything and no amount of parental discipline seemed to make him behave properly for long. At the age of six he set a fire in his father's barn, "just to see what it would do," he said. He received a public whipping from his father in the village square for this, but such whippings failed to make him conform to accepted behavior.

Young Al seemed to be different from other children, and he made only a few friends. He did poorly in school, and his teachers didn't believe he had much intelligence. They didn't appear to notice that he had a great curiosity about everything. Although he was bored with school lessons, he was eager to learn how things worked. What's more, he wanted to find out for himself by experimenting. For example, when he saw that rubbing a cat's fur would produce static electricity, he tied the tails of two tomcats together with a wire and rubbed their fur vigorously, hoping to produce an electric current. All he got for his trouble were some bloody scratches from the angry cats.

Only his mother sensed that he had a high degree of intelligence. Although she kept a birch switch in the kitchen and whipped him with it frequently, she also gave him good books to read and encouraged his lively curiosity. She gave him books by Shakespeare and Charles Dickens and discussed them with him. When he was nine, she presented him with a science textbook, *Parker's School of Natural Philosophy,* which explained chemical experiments that could be conducted at home. This was exactly what the boy wanted, and he read it from cover to cover, fascinated with every page.

Young Edison soon set up a laboratory in a corner of the cellar of the house in Port Huron, Michigan, where the family had moved. He asked local store owners for bottles that were about to be thrown out, and he used these for storing his chemicals. Eventually he had about 200 of them, each filled with a different chemical. He repeated the experiments described in Parker's textbook, learning by trial and error. Occasionally there were small explosions, and sometimes terrible odors came from the basement. But his parents generally encouraged him with his experiments, because they realized this avid interest kept him out of trouble.

When he was eleven, the boy raised a considerable amount of money by growing and selling vegetables. He immediately spent this money to build his own telegraph system with a neighbor boy. Samuel F. B. Morse had invented the telegraph only a short time before, and this exciting new system was a big advance in communications. Edison and his friend ran a line between their houses. Learning the Morse code, they tapped messages to each other far into the night. Other neighborhood children became interested, and soon there were lines forming a network between several houses. Edison had a natural gift for sending and receiving the code; and he often became impatient when his friends were unable to follow his high-speed messages. The local telegraph system came to an end when a stray cow knocked down a pole in the Edison yard one night and got tangled up in the wire. Before the animal was freed, it had wrecked the telegraph system completely.

By the time he was twelve, Edison felt he was ready to go to work and earn a living. Since he cared little for school and his father had scarcely enough money to support him anyway, his parents agreed to let him get a job. In 1859, the law did not require a child to attend school until the age of sixteen, as it generally does today. He promptly got a job on the Grand Trunk Railway line, selling newspapers, candy, apples and sandwiches. He worked on the morning train, which left Port Huron at seven each day and reached Detroit about three hours later. The train would remain there most of the day while freight was loaded, then it would make the return trip, reaching Port Huron at 9:30 p.m. It made a long workday, and Edison had several hours of free time in Detroit every day while waiting for the return trip. He asked the train master for permission to set up his home laboratory in a corner of the baggage car, and the train master agreed.

Edison was happy with this arrangement, which allowed him to earn money and carry on his experiments. He showed a good business sense from the start. He began selling fruit, vegetables and other local produce from Port Huron to passengers on the morning train. Business grew so swiftly that he soon had other boys working for him and his profit reached twenty dollars per week.

The experiments in the baggage car went well until a couple of years later, when a sudden lurch in the train caused some phosphorus he was using to ignite, setting off a small fire in the car. The conductor asked him to remove his laboratory equipment and chemicals from the train after that.

Edison began to go deaf not long after he started his train job. It was an affliction that would trouble him the rest of his life, his hearing getting progressively worse over the years. An early case of scarlet fever may have been part of the cause, but it was never determined. Later in life, Edison told of an injury to his ears that he felt caused his hearing loss. He was late getting to the train one day, and it started to pull out of the station without him. He wrote: "I ran after it and caught the rear step nearly out of wind and hardly able to lift myself up, for the steps in those days were high. A trainman reached and grabbed me by the ears, and as he pulled me up, I felt something in my ears crack; right after that I began to get deaf . . . If it was that man who injured my hearing, he did it while saving my life."

Edison's difficulty in hearing made it hard for him to enjoy the companionship of other people, so he turned more within himself for amusement. He began a campaign of self-education, reading for hours at a library in Detroit while waiting for the return train trip to Port Huron. He read many classic books, by such authors as Victor Hugo, Isaac New-

[85]

ton and Robert Burton. He found Newton's book on mathematics, *Principia,* very difficult. "It gave me a distaste for mathematics from which I have never recovered," he said later. Yet he was very capable of understanding mathematics.

Always restless and ambitious, the boy next decided to publish his own newspaper aboard the train. He bought a small, second-hand printing press and installed it in the baggage car. The newspaper, the *Weekly Herald,* was entirely produced by Edison. He wrote all the stories, set them in type and ran them off on his press, selling the newspapers on the train for three cents a copy. The paper's circulation soon rose to five hundred, producing a profit of about forty-five dollars a month.

Before long, Edison lost interest in the paper because his old enthusiasm for telegraphy was revived. Again he and a friend constructed a telegraph line, this one stretching a half mile. It was not long after, in 1862, that he moved into professional telegraphy. It happened because he was waiting for a train at a station and saw a three-year-old boy wander onto the track when a train was approaching. Young Edison grabbed the child and carried him to safety. The boy's grateful father, who happened to be an experienced telegraph operator, offered to teach Edison the professional method of telegraphy.

Edison gave up his train job and spent five months learning to send and receive messages the professional way. He learned so well that he got a job as night telegraph operator at the Port Huron station. On this night job he had had plenty of free time to read scientific magazines, experiment with electrical circuits he designed and practice his telegraphy skill.

A couple of years later, he took another telegraphy job as a railroad dispatcher at Stratford Junction, Ontario, about forty miles from Port Huron. He worked a twelve-hour night shift, handling messages and confirming train arrivals and departures. There weren't many trains at night, and Edison had trouble staying awake. The railroad had a rule that each station operator must signal the main office at certain hours during the night shift, just to prove that he was awake. Edison soon put his mechanical ingenuity to work so that he could get some sleep during the long, dull nights. He designed a revolving wheel attached to a clock that automatically sent a signal to the main office at the correct hours. It was his first real invention, although he had to keep it a secret from his bosses.

By the time he was seventeen, Edison had begun a sort of nomadic life, drifting from one telegraphy job to another. This was quite common at the time, for the demand of the nation's expanding telegraph system for operators was huge. An experienced operator could go nearly anywhere and find a job. The jobs didn't pay well, but they were plentiful. He moved to Toledo, Ohio; Fort Wayne, Indiana; Indianapolis, and then Cincinnati, Ohio. Edison proved to be an excellent operator; he could send and receive faster than most others. He was also interested in how the telegraph machines worked, and he began to produce innovations of his own. One was a device for recording messages as they came in. It was an impressive invention for a teenage boy, but he couldn't persuade his supervisors to use it.

Generally, he didn't get along with supervisors. He was too imaginative and unwilling to accept discipline, and he was frequently fired from jobs. His old childhood habit of playing pranks kept getting him into trouble, too. In those days before office water fountains, a pail and a dipper were used if workers wanted a drink of water. Once Edison wired the dipper to a battery, which caused the workers to receive a shock when they touched it.

Edison continued moving from one Western Union office to another. He worked in Memphis, then Louisville, Kentucky. At each place he continued to experiment with the telegraph equipment whenever he could find free time. In Louisville, he tried to devise a duplex telegraph—one that could send two messages over a single wire at the same time. This would double the capacity of the company's lines—an immensely valuable invention. He secretly experimented with the equipment in the office at night, but when the station manager found out, he was angry and made Edison stop his experiments. Not long afterward, a Boston inventor named J. B. Stearns took out a patent for a duplex telegraph device. Edison felt certain he could have been first with the invention if he had been allowed to continue his experiments.

Next he took a telegraph operator's job in Boston. He spent much of his free time there browsing in bookstores. In one of them he found a two-volume set that had a great impact on him: *Experimental Researches in Electricity,* by Michael Farady, an early experimenter in the field. Edison found the author's explanations of electricity clear and inspiring. He repeated many of Faraday's experiments in his spare time, borrowing space in a shop. Excitedly, he told a friend, "I am now twenty-one. I may live to be fifty. Can I get as much done as he did? I have got so much to do and life is so short that I am going to hustle."

And he did. After quitting his job, he devoted his full time to inventing a telegraphic vote-recording machine. He believed it could be useful to Congress, state legislatures and other organizations, saving time in counting votes. He was granted a patent on the machine in 1869, the first of more than a thousand patents he was to receive. Edison borrowed money for a trip to Washington, D.C., where he demonstrated the device to a committee of Congressmen. But the Congressmen did not feel they needed such a machine.

It was a crushing disappointment to the young inventor, but it taught him something. It wasn't enough to invent something out of pure scientific interest. "Of course I was very sorry," Edison said of the experience, "for I had banked on that machine bringing me in money. But it was a lesson to me. There and then I made a vow that I would never invent anything which was not wanted, or which was not necessary to the community at large."

Next he invented an improved duplex telegraph machine, hoping to go a step further than the man who had beat him out on his first try at it. But when he arranged a demonstration, the machine failed miserably. Success in his career as an inventor seemed a long way off. Borrowing a few dollars, he set out for New York City, hoping his luck would change in that city.

It did, after he took another job running a stock ticker machine. This type of machine was useful to financial buyers and sellers because it provided on a tape the latest prices of gold and securities. As usual, Edison began tinkering with the machine, finding ways to make it work better. He soon applied for and received a number of patents for improved ticker machines.

Western Union had asked him to work on some improvements for the machines, and now they wanted to buy the patent rights from him. He thought of asking them for $5,000, but was afraid it might be too much. Instead, he said, "Suppose you make me an offer?" To his amazement, the reply was, "How would $40,000 strike you?" Gulping, the startled inventor said that figure would be fine.

At last, he had the break he needed to be a full-time inventor. Western Union ordered one thousand, two hundred of the improved tickers, to be manufactured over several years. The order amounted to nearly a half million dollars of business. Edison rented some space in Newark, New Jersey, and converted it into a machine shop. He hired eighteen men, who had the proper backgrounds and training for the demanding work ahead. At the age of twenty-four, Edison was younger than most of his staff assistants. He was involved in the daily work of the shop as much as any of the workers, with no job too lowly for the owner. "He was as dirty as any of the other workmen, and not much better dressed than a tramp," one of them said later.

While the manufacturing was going on, Edison was busy inventing at the same time. He was awarded thirty-eight patents in 1872 and twenty-five more the next year. By 1876 he had been granted more than two hundred patents, for such things as telegraph printers, relay magnets and stock ticker improvements. He changed the basic approach to invention, which up to that time had been done by loners, working by themselves. Instead, he developed a team approach, with his staff assistants working on his ideas. It was the forerunner of today's industrial research laboratories.

Edison worked long hours, and he expected his staff to do the same. He would often work all day and all through the night if a project needed to be completed. Surprisingly, he met with little objection from his staff. His enthusiasm spread to them, too, and they became as determined as he to complete each invention. He was capable of going long days and nights without sleep. He often caught "cat naps" on a desk or bench, or on the floor—just enough sleep to keep him going for several hours more.

He soon had a major success on his hands—the invention of the quadruplex telegraph system, which could send and receive *four* messages at the same time, doubling the capability of the duplex machine. It was this invention that made him famous.

The duplex telegraph system could send two messages one way on a wire, but by manipulating the electrical current, Edison found a way to send two more messages in the other direction at the same time. This doubling, once again, of the capability of the telegraph system, was worth a lot of money to the telegraph companies. Edison had gone to the head of Western Union and offered to develop the quadruplex system. He had been promised financial backing, but when the company delayed paying him, he took his invention to a rival company, Automatic Telegraph, and sold it. This started a long and widely publicized legal battle between the two companies over the rights to use Edison's patents. The newspaper accounts of the struggle over the invention made Edison's name prominent throughout the country.

At about the same time, he had also perfected an automatic telegraph, which made use of a moving paper tape to transmit and receive messages at a very high speed. Edison sold the patent he obtained on this device to Automatic Telegraph. He was also busily engaged in inventing and patenting a number of advancements in telegraphy technology for Western Union. Eventually Wall Street financier Jay Gould, who owned Automatic Telegraph, bought out Western Union and merged the companies into a new one called Western Union. As payment for the services he provided with his inventions, Edison was supposed to receive stock in Gould's company, but he was cheated out of it, according to his account. He sued, but the case dragged on for an incredible thirty years and by then, he no longer needed the money.

Despite his frantic work pace, Edison found time to fall in love with one of the employees in his New Jersey shop, a sixteen-year-old girl named Mary Stilwell. She was a gentle girl of simple tastes, who saw her genius employer as a hero. They were married in 1871. She saw little of her husband because he continued working up to eighteen hours a day, yet they had a genuine love for each other that made up for his difficult schedule. Her patience and understanding gave him the emotional support he needed to meet the challenges he was facing.

Edison's creative ability seemed boundless in these early years. He invented a telegraphic burglar alarm and sold the patent outright. He devised an electric pen, powered by a small motor, which cut through paper to form stencils that could be used to run off many copies. This led, in 1875, to his invention of the mimeograph, a "device for multiplying copies of letters," which was used for a century afterward in offices and is still seen today. He sold the patent rights for this to the A.B. Dick Company of Chicago.

By now, Edison was getting tired of running a manufacturing operation at the same time that he was working on his inventions. His Newark factory was manufacturing many small devices he had invented, but running a business took a large part of his time. Now that he had achieved some fame and success, he wanted to get out of manufacturing completely and devote himself exclusively to inventing. He figured he could earn a good income by selling licensing rights for his inventions to large corporations. Under such arrangements, they would pay him for the rights to manufacture the things he invented, but he wouldn't be involved in manufacturing them himself.

What he wanted was a place in the country where he could pursue his research projects in peaceful surroundings. He found such a spot on top of a hill in Menlo Park, New Jersey, about twenty-five miles from New York City. There were only about a half-dozen houses in Menlo Park, so he was assured of seclusion. He sold the Newark factory and purchased the hilltop site in 1876. Next, he asked his father to come from Michigan to take charge of the construction of his new laboratory—a request that delighted his father, who was very proud of his son's success.

The laboratory was a wooden building that looked like a barn, a hundred feet long and thirty feet wide, painted white. A picket fence was installed around the building to keep wandering cows and horses out. Edison took all the money he had from the sale of the Newark factory and used it to buy the finest scientific material for the laboratory. Horse-drawn wagons delivered a steam engine, a gaslight apparatus, tools, instruments, chemicals of all sorts, batteries and wire.

He also took the key assistants he had worked with in Newark to his new operation. These fifteen or so men had unique talents for making his ideas into working devices, and they were very valuable to him. Most of them were so loyal that they worked for him for many years, caught up in the same enthusiasm he felt for his work.

Edison's ambitions for his new research center were big. He said he wanted to turn out "a minor invention every ten days and a big thing every six months or so." The first big project at Menlo Park was a request from Western Union to develop a "speaking telegraph"—a telephone, that is. Alexander Graham Bell had beaten him to it, however, filing for a patent on his telephone in February 1876. But Bell's telephone had at least one major problem. The receiver was satisfactory, but the transmitter was poor and a human voice could not be heard very well, especially if the distance was great. The machine simply didn't have the power to transmit a voice sound very far.

Edison set to work and came up with an entirely different concept for a transmitter and speaker. His transmitting system used small granules of carbon to control the flow of electrical current through a vibrating metal diaphragm. He filed for a patent on it in April 1877. The following year, Western Union conducted a demonstration of Edison's system that was a huge success. Voices could be heard clearly and loudly over a line 107 miles long between New York City and Philadelphia. The carbon device worked perfectly.

Edison's transmitter was better than Bell's, but his receiver was not as effective. The logical thing to do was to combine the two systems for the best telephone, and eventually this was done. Western Union sold its telephone interests, including Edison's patent, to the Bell Telephone Company, which had been formed by Bell's financial backers. Now Edison's transmitter could legally be used with Bell's receiver. Thus Edison made an important contribution to the development of the telephone.

His work on the telephone project interested him in another idea—the phonograph. Working with a telephone receiver diaphragm, Edison wondered if its vibrations might be used in a different way. His idea was to have a vibrating diaphragm, following recorded instructions, reproduce sound. At this stage, he did not envision the phonograph of today, used to play recorded music, but thought of it as a useful business machine. A person could dictate a message into a machine, and the voice could be heard on the machine later.

His first effort was to use rolls of paper coated with paraffin, pulling them along a diaphragm that had a pin mounted in it. When a person spoke into the diaphragm, the pin cut a groove into the paper.

Then when the paper was pulled along under another diaphragm, a faint sound was played back. But the sound wasn't good enough to be useful, so Edison put in painstaking hours of work, experimenting with other materials.

He found that tinfoil worked better, so he drew a sketch of a phonograph machine and asked one of his assistants to make the model for him. On this machine, a needle cut grooves into tinfoil wrapped around a cylinder, which was turned by a hand crank.

When the brass and iron device was ready for his test, Edison wrapped the foil around the cylinder, began turning the handle, and spoke into a tube connected to the diaphragm. He recited the nursery jingle, "Mary had a little lamb." Then, as several of his workmen watched, he returned the cylinder to the starting point and cranked the handle again. As the needle traveled over the grooves in the foil, the faint sound of Edison's voice reciting the nursery rhyme was clearly heard. The workmen were stunned—it worked! It seemed like a miracle to them, and Edison was astounded, too. He said later, "I was never so taken aback in my life."

It was an amazing development. Never in the history of mankind had the spoken word been preserved, to hear again and again. Edison and his assistants were so delighted that they stayed up until dawn, singing, whistling and talking into the machine, then playing it back.

Edison was granted a patent for the phonograph

in 1877. The Patent Office examiners found that this was an absolutely new invention, and that no one had ever attempted to patent a machine to record and play back sound before.

This was an invention the public could appreciate, and the newspapers and magazines of the country wrote many articles about the phonograph and its inventor. One paper called Edison "the Wizard of Menlo Park," and this became a popular nickname for him. He was invited to demonstrate his machine to members of the U.S. Senate in Washington. Late one evening, after he had played the machine for senators and cabinet ministers, word came that President Rutherford B. Hayes wanted to see the machine. Arriving at the White House after eleven o'clock, Edison entertained the President and his guests until three o'clock in the morning.

Edison realized, however, that the phonograph needed a lot of work and improvements before it would be commercially successful. The tinfoil wore out quickly, and the sounds were not good enough for such uses as enjoying music. He experimented with wax cylinders instead of tinfoil, and he also tried making disk-shaped wax records. But there were technical difficulties with these and mechanical improvements would be needed in the diaphragm and the needle. It would require several years of slow, patient experimentation to perfect the machine, and Edison was impatient to get on with other ideas he had in mind.

He lost interest in the phonograph and dropped

his work in it for nearly a decade. The wonderful machine rested in his laboratory storage room while he concentrated on other inventions, including one that was to be even more important: the incandescent electric light.

Edison was not the first inventor to experiment with electric lights. A type of lamp called the arc light was already in operation in some parts of Europe and the United States in the 1870s. Electric generators, called dynamos, were used to generate limited power for these lights, which were used mainly as street lights. In the electric arc light, two small rods of carbon placed close together were burned by electric current. This set up a burning arc between them, which was extremely bright. In fact, it was so bright that looking at this light was painful to the eyes. Consequently the arc light was only useful in an outdoor location or a very large hall.

Edison hadn't been very interested in the electric light, but he was urged by an attorney friend to turn his talents to finding a form of electric light that would be more useful. Although arc lights were being hailed as the lights of the future, Edison saw that that future would be very limited. Gas lights were then very much in use in cities, where gas companies had installed gas lines to homes and business buildings. But gas lights had limitations. The illumination they gave was dim and flickering, and they required some form of venting to eliminate the residue of gas combustion.

Thomas A. Edison as a young man. Before he was thirty, Edison had already tried and failed to perfect and sell a number of inventions. He also received his first big break before that age, winning a large manufacturing contract from Western Union for an improved stock ticker machine. (Photo courtesy of Edison National Historic Site)

A drawing of Edison's Menlo Park, New Jersey laboratory complex around 1880. The incandescent electric light bulb, the phonograph and an amazing number of other inventions were produced in this modest workplace. The laboratory can be seen today at Greenfield Village, Dearborn, Michigan, where Henry Ford moved it to add to a collection of historic buildings. (Photo courtesy of Edison National Historic Site)

Thomas Edison's original phonograph, invented in 1877. By turning the crank, a needle was put in contact with the cylinder grooves, producing sound through the pipelike speaker. (Photo courtesy of Edison National Historic Site)

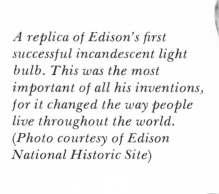

A replica of Edison's first successful incandescent light bulb. This was the most important of all his inventions, for it changed the way people live throughout the world. (Photo courtesy of Edison National Historic Site)

Edison experimenting with an improved version of the phonograph using wax cylinders, 1888. It was said that this photograph was taken after Edison had worked round-the-clock for two days and was exhausted. (Photo courtesy of Edison National Historic Site)

Thomas Edison in his chemical laboratory at West Orange, New Jersey in 1906. By this time he was wealthy and famous, but he continued to work long hours, doing many of his own experiments. (Photo courtesy of Edison National Historic Site)

Other inventors in the United States and England were working on something they called the incandescent lamp. Incandescent means "to grow hot and to glow," and it was hoped that a lamp could be created that would do that from an electric current. It would be a softer light than arc lights provided and could be used in a home or in an office. But no one had been able to find the right material to glow steadily while burning with an electric current.

Edison pondered the problem after reading all the material he could get on arc lights and electric lighting in general. To put electric light in every room of millions of homes, a whole new system of electric power generation and distribution would be required. The size and scope of such a project was almost beyond imagination and most scientists declared it to be impossible. It was one thing to generate and distribute power for a limited number of arc lights in a local area, but how could it be done for millions of homes? Also, an arc light required enormous amounts of electric current. If an incandescent type of light needed a similar quantity of voltage, it would be impossible to produce and distribute enough power.

Edison considered these problems before deciding whether he should try to perfect an incandescent bulb. First, to reduce the amount of power that needed to be generated, a way would have to be found to subdivide high voltage currents into smaller amounts of electricity for each home or building. Second, an incandescent light system would have to have high resistance to electric current, which in effect would turn away the unneeded amounts of electricity and use only enough to light the lamps. A complete system of power generation and distribution would have to be created to accomplish this, or perfecting an incandescent light would be a waste of time.

The magnitude of Edison's achievement can be seen when one realizes that these problems seemed insurmountable and yet he solved them. The problem of distributing electric current through wires to city homes could be solved by running the wires and main cables through existing gas lines, he believed. He was convinced that electricity could be generated through steam power in new dynamos that would achieve up to ninety percent efficiency, replacing the dynamos then in use, which wasted more than half their energy in operation. Experts said this couldn't be done, but Edison's confidence never wavered. After some experimentation, he felt he could design a high-resistance device for the incandescent lamp, to reduce the amount of current it would need. And if these were accomplished, he was confident that he could find a method of transmitting a steady, low-voltage current of electricity to all the homes and buildings connected to the system.

Edison said later that his vision of the entire electrical system came to him all at once. He wrote:

"Means and ways had to be devised for maintaining an even voltage everywhere on the system. The lamps nearest the dynamo had to receive the same current as the lamps farthest away. The burning out or breaking of lamps must not affect those remaining in the circuit, and means had to be provided to prevent violent fluctuations of current.

"One of the largest problems of all was that I had to build dynamos more efficient and larger than any then made. Many electrical people stated that the *internal* resistance of the armature should be equal to the external resistance; but I made up my mind that I wanted to sell all the electricity I made and not waste half in the machine, so I made my internal resistance small and got out ninety percent of salable energy.

"Over and above these things, many other devices had to be invented and perfected, such as devices to prevent excessive currents, proper switching gear, lamp holders, chandeliers and all manner of details that were necessary to make a complete system of electric lighting that could compete successfully with the gas system. Such was the work to be done in the early part of 1878. The task was enormous, but we put our shoulders to the wheel, and in a year and a half we had a system of electrical lighting that was a success. During this period, I had upwards of one hundred energetic men working hard on all details."

While work was progressing on all these challenges, Edison turned his talent toward designing an incandescent bulb. The reason for wanting a bulb of glass was so that he could have his incandescent material burn in a vacuum. With air present, any material would burn too fast and would have to be replaced frequently. He wanted a slow, dependable burning, so the light would last a long time. He and his assistants used special pumps to remove the air from glass bulbs, creating a vacuum.

The greatest problem was finding a suitable material to burn. Working night and day, Edison and his staff tried dozens of different materials. He began with carbon-coated paper strips a sixteenth of an inch wide. He was able to keep these burning for eight minutes, which was not satisfactory. Then he tried a variety of metals—platinum, titanium, rhodium and others. He applied for a patent on an incandescent bulb using platinum, but he doubted that this was the real answer because platinum's melting point was only slightly above the point at which it reached incandescence, causing frequent burnouts. He continued the search, also bearing in mind that his lamp would have to be a high-resistance device to cut down on the electricity needed.

By now, Edison fully appreciated the value of publicity in attracting the attention of big investors on Wall Street. If they read enough about him and his progress, they would be more interested in investing money to build the system he had in mind. He knew it would require a lot of money, and he wanted to get his financial backing while he was still working on the invention of the system. So he gave interviews to the press that were full of confidence, stating that he expected to have the revolutionary new system perfected soon.

His efforts worked. By October 1878, J. P. Morgan, W. H. Vanderbilt and a number of other wealthy investors agreed to put up the money to establish the Edison Electric Light Company, which would produce and operate the electric light system. In return for $50,000 in cash and two thousand five hundred shares of stock, which could make him a millionaire if the company were successful, Edison agreed to give the company the rights to all his inventions in electric light systems over the next five years. The company would also manufacture the materials and devices needed for the system. Now that he had the financial backing to build the system, Edison went ahead with confidence in his research.

The search for the ideal burning material continued. Edison adopted the word "filament" to describe the material. He knew he had to find one that would reach incandescence without requiring great amounts of electric current. In other words, a high-resistance burner. He was still working with platinum wire, a very expensive metal, and his costs were so great that he soon used up the $50,000 he had received from his backers in the Edison Electric Light Company. A group of these wealthy men came to Menlo Park for a demonstration of the electric lights he was working on. But the demonstration was a failure—the lights kept burning out. This discouraged the financiers, and they began to talk about putting a limit on any more money they would advance him.

A disappointed Edison decided to give up on

the platinum filament. He went back to carbon and he tried carbonized celluloid, coconut shells, wood shavings, fish line, cork, cotton lamp wick and many types of paper. The complexity of the challenge was enormous, because there was little prior knowledge to go on. In a newspaper interview, Edison described the challenge: "Just consider this. We have an almost infinitesimal filament heated to a degree which it is difficult to comprehend, and it is in a vacuum under conditions of which we are wholly ignorant. You cannot use your eyes to help you, and you really know nothing of what is going on in that tiny bulb. I speak without exaggeration when I say that I have constructed three thousand different theories in connection with the electric light, each of them reasonable and apparently likely to be true. Yet in two cases only did my experiments prove the truth of my theories."

Edison's calculations showed that a carbon filament, in order to have the desired high-resistance characteristic, should be no more than a sixty-fourth of an inch in diameter. He began carbonizing sewing thread. He put the thread in an earthenware vessel, covered it with powdered carbon and "baked" it for several hours. The charred thread was wired to the stem assembly of a lamp and then a glass globe was put over it. After a vacuum was created in the globe with a pump, it was tested. The filament was so delicate that on the first eight tries it broke before the test could begin.

In October 1879, Edison and his assistant worked

on this project all one night, the next day, and the next night again. Finally, on the following day, they had the ninth lamp ready for testing. Cautiously, he turned the current on, and as he put it, "the sight we had so long desired to see met our eyes." The incandescent bulb burned steadily. The current was increased, and it still burned. Edison and his staff watched it all that night. A second bulb was lighted and it continued burning for forty hours, proving at last that an incandescent light was feasible.

"I think we've got it," Edison said. "If it can burn forty hours, I can make it last a hundred."

Within two weeks, he filed for a patent on his incandescent light. Calling his invention "an improvement in electric lamps," he explained in his application, "The object of this invention is to produce electric lamps giving light by incandescence, which lamps shall have high resistance, so as to allow of the practical subdivision of the electric light."

This patent, Number 223,898, was granted on January 27, 1880. Of all the patents he was granted in his lifetime, this was the most significant, for it was the cornerstone of his entire electrical system that transformed the world. It was for this patent that Edison was later inducted into the National Inventors Hall of Fame, the first inventor honored by that institution.

At the time, however, Edison hardly had time to pause for honors. Caught up in the excitement of his discovery, he rushed into one experiment after another to improve on his success. Soon he returned to the first filament material he had tried: carbonized paper. Now he was able to make filaments with it that burned for one hundred and seventy hours, and he was sure he could make bulbs that would burn for a thousand hours in the future. He and his staff tried many different shapes and sizes of bulbs, as well as turning out duplicates of the original successful bulb.

These bulbs were soon hanging in the laboratory, in Edison's house and in some nearby boarding houses, strung on wires connected to the generator at the laboratory. Next, lights were strung along the streets of Menlo Park.

Crowds of visitors were soon making the journey to the little town to see the lights, and newspaper and magazine stories described them to the nation. When Edison announced that his laboratory would be open to the public for a week, special trains were put into service between New York City and Menlo Park. The demonstration proved to the public that the incandescent lamp really worked, and it created a desire in many people for this new form of lighting.

The revolution that the inventor had triggered was off to a fast start. Within a year, he had produced a bulb that lasted 1,589 hours, and the demand grew as the electrical system became installed. In 1882, one hundred thousand bulbs were made. A decade later, more than four million a year were being produced.

Work rushed ahead on the design and production of new, powerful dynamos to supply the current needed. In 1881, Edison obtained permission from the government of New York City to build and install an electrical lighting system covering one square mile of lower Manhattan. However, his backers in the Edison Electric Light Company grew timid when it came time to invest millions of dollars in factories to manufacture the material and equipment that would be needed. Edison promptly set up three companies of his own to manufacture the goods, raising the money by selling some of his shares in Edison Electric and by borrowing heavily. In the meantime, a central power station was personally designed by Edison and built on Pearl Street in New York City. In 1882, electric service began, the first in the United States from a central power plant.

By this time, Edison had moved with his family to New York City. He had three children: daughter Marion, born in 1872, Thomas A. Edison Jr., born in 1876, and William, born in 1878. They continued to use their house in Menlo Park as a summer home, and it was there, in the summer of 1884, that his wife contracted typhoid fever and died.

Her sudden death was a shattering blow to Edison. Although he had been too busy to spend much time with his wife and children, he treasured those times when he could. His wife had been a source of comfort and stability to him.

In his grief, the inventor plunged into work. But the spark of youthful enthusiasm seemed to be gone. He moved all his operations out of Menlo Park, the scene of his greatest achievements, and allowed the buildings to fall into ruin.

But his business prospered as the electrical system he invented continued to expand around the country. His manufacturing firms made large profits as they turned out the bulbs, sockets, and all the attendant equipment needed as the country turned to electricity. He licensed his system in Europe, too. Many of today's electric utilities in the United States are direct descendents of the companies Edison formed to supply electric service to cities around the country.

In 1886, Edison married Mina Miller, the daughter of a successful Ohio industrialist and a well-educated woman. In keeping with his status as a famous and wealthy inventor and businessman, he bought an impressive mansion in West Orange, New Jersey, for them to live in. The twenty-three-room house was surrounded by beautiful gardens. A half mile away, he built a whole new complex of laboratories, the largest and best-equipped laboratory facility in the world at the time. It consisted of five brick buildings and had a staff of about fifty working on research.

Edison continued to invent things for the electrical industry, compiling a total of one hundred sixty-eight patents in this field after his famous one for the incandescent light. Later, he also perfected the phonograph, and he made such great improvements in it that it soon became a commercial success.

He established the Edison Phonograph Company, which became the national leader in manufacturing phonographs and was also successful in making phonograph records.

At about this time many inventors in the United States and Europe were trying to create a system for projecting motion pictures, but no one had the solution. In experiments at his West Orange laboratories, Edison and his staff made a series of tiny negatives on a sensitized cylinder that was moved between each exposure. The result was a spiral of small pictures that gave the illusion of movement when viewed under a microscope.

Edison called his device a "kinetoscope." The biggest drawback was that the glass-plate method by which photographs were made created a blurry image. When Edison heard that George Eastman had invented a new type of flexible film for still cameras, he wrote to him and asked for a supply of this film. It would be just the thing for a motion picture system, he felt. He concentrated on a strip of film, with pictures appearing in sequence, one after another. A fifty-foot band of this film on a spool or reel powered by an electric motor could be pulled beneath a viewing glass, giving the illusion of movement. Edison designed a machine for this, a sort of "peep show" box that was activated by putting a coin in a slot. He patented it in 1891, and it soon became a commercially successful device, popular with the public.

At the same time, he worked on the development of a screen-projection system, such as we have today in theaters, as well as the movie camera. He even established the world's first movie studio at West Orange and filmed dramatic and musical presentations. He experimented with recording sound to go with the film images—the world's first "talkies." He had little trouble synchronizing sound with the film. The difficulty with sound was the inability of phonograph microphones at the time to pick up sounds more than a few feet away. As a result, it would be years before talking motion pictures would be a practical reality. But Edison's work on the motion picture was the basis of the future development of movies.

Edison bowed out of the manufacturing business when he sold his interests in his firms to the Edison General Electric Company, formed in a merger with his old companies. The money he got assured him of wealth, and he retained ten percent of the stock in Edison General Electric. Later, this company was merged again with another firm, and Edison was paid for his remaining share. The new company was called General Electric Company, and although Edison was on the board of directors, he no longer was an influential owner.

Edison's later years seemed to be less productive than his first forty years, but perhaps this is only because he had accomplished almost superhuman feats before. He continued to experiment on a wide variety of projects, including an idea for an electric automobile and a method of making synthetic rubber for automobile tires from goldenrod plants. He became friends with other industrial geniuses such as Henry Ford and Harvey Firestone, with whom he went on long camping trips.

As the years went by, Edison became a sort of folk hero to Americans and to people in foreign countries as well. He was awarded scores of medals and citations for his great achievements and was much sought-after as an honored dinner guest and speaker. He was easily the most famous inventor in history, and he appeared to enjoy his fame.

When Henry Ford built a recreated historical community in Michigan called Greenfield Village, he bought the decaying laboratory buildings at Menlo Park and moved them to the historical exhibit, so the public could see the buildings where "the Wizard of Menlo Park" had made his great inventions.

Greenfield Village was ready to be inaugurated in 1929, which also happened to be the year America was celebrating the fiftieth anniversary of the invention of the incandescent light bulb. Henry Ford asked his old friend if he would come to a gala celebration as the guest of honor, and Edison gratefully accepted. President Herbert Hoover and a host of other prominent people would also attend the celebration, called Light's Golden Jubilee.

Edison was eighty-two years old and in frail health. He arrived in Michigan somewhat exhausted by his trip from New Jersey. But his spirits revived when he saw the restored Menlo Park. He smiled broadly as he toured the old laboratory, the machine shop and the library, recognizing his bulbs, electrical equipment and dynamos. He was amazed that everything had been restored so carefully.

Turning to Ford, he said, "Henry, it's ninety-nine and nine-tenths perfect."

"Well, where did we make a mistake?" Ford asked.

"Our floor was never as clean as this," Edison replied.

At the conclusion of all the festivities and the ceremonial banquet, the old inventor said, "I am tired of glory. I want to get back to work."

And this is what he did, returning to his New Jersey laboratories to experiment further with his synthetic rubber project. But time, at last, was running out on this great genius. His health began to fail even more, and in 1931 he collapsed from a variety of medical problems. For several weeks he rested in the bedroom of his beloved West Orange home, alternately getting better and then suffering relapses. When the end finally came, he died peacefully.

The nation—indeed, much of the world—mourned the loss of this man who had brought so much improvement to people's lives. By giving the world light, electricity, the phonograph and movies, he had played a larger part in the making of modern America than any other single person.

It was suggested at the time of his death that the nation could best pay honor to his remarkable contributions by shutting off all electric power for one minute. But it was soon realized that the country would be crippled if the power distribution system were cut off, even for that length of time. Within half a century, his life had altered the world so completely that no other tribute was needed.

Today, Edison's home and laboratory in West Orange, New Jersey, are a part of the Edison National Historic Site, open to the public. One can also see his reconstructed Menlo Park laboratory at Greenfield Village in Dearborn, Michigan. There have been many tributes to his genius by the electric power companies and by museums. And each one of us pays unconscious tribute to him every day, simply by turning a light switch. Undoubtedly, that tribute would satisfy him more than any other.

GEORGE EASTMAN

The Man Who Made Photography Popular

HISTORY is filled with stories of inventors who created useful things for mankind, but whose talents did not include the business ability to manufacture those products. Many of these inventors had to leave the job of producing and distributing their products to people skilled in industry. Some sold their patents outright; others, if they weren't careful to protect their ideas through patents, failed to earn any money from their inventions.

This was not the case with George Eastman, the man who did more than anyone else to make photography available to everyone at a reasonable cost. Eastman not only invented cameras and films that were easy to use, but he invented an entire system for developing and printing pictures and built machinery to produce the material needed. He went on to build the Eastman Kodak Company into a huge, successful business.

Before Eastman made his innovations, photography was an expensive, cumbersome undertaking limited to professionals who could afford it. The heavy cameras of that time were placed on tripods or tables. Pictures were taken on glass plates, and these plates had to be coated with liquid silver nitrate solutions before they were exposed. The silver nitrate solution had to be carried to the scene where pictures were taken, and a portable "darkroom" tent had to be carried also, for the glass plates had to be developed immediately.

Eastman changed all that with his small, lightweight Kodak cameras that held flexible, transparent film on rolls. One of the first American manufacturers to use modern mass production methods, he was able to make his cameras and film cheaply enough so that millions of people could afford them. As a result, "snapshots" became a popular part of American life nearly a century ago. Family photo albums became a tradition, recording events such as weddings, graduations, holidays and vacations. Eastman's film also made motion pictures possible. We tend to take these for granted, but our ancestors didn't have them. It took the talent and ambition of George Eastman to enable us to freeze people, moments and events with a camera.

Eastman was born at Waterville, New York, in July 1854. He was the third child and only son of George W. and Maria Eastman, who lived in a small, one-story frame house. At that time Waterville was a town of only a few hundred people, surrounded by farming country. George's father operated his own business college in nearby Rochester, New York. Named Eastman's Commercial College, it was the first school of its type to use actual business cases in its studies, rather than textbook theories. Most of the students were trained to become bookkeepers and accountants. It wasn't the sort of enterprise that would make its founder rich, but George W. Eastman was able to provide a comfortable living for his wife and children.

When young George was six, his father moved the family to Rochester so he would be closer to his work. But the family's comfortable life came to a tragic end two years after the move, when his father died. From that point on, his childhood was spent in poverty as his mother struggled to raise her three children on what little income she could get by taking in boarders. This experience created a drive and ambition in the boy to rise above poverty, and he worked at spare-time jobs to earn money with every chance he got. He opened his first bank account while he was still in grade school, depositing five dollars he had earned by cutting wood. He took pride in being able to earn his own money, and he was determined to earn more.

George left school before he was fourteen, to take a full-time job as a messenger at an insurance agency in Rochester. The pay was only three dollars a week, but he considered it an opportunity to start a career in the business world. His mother agreed, because the money he could give her would help the family to survive. George had a close and affectionate relationship with his mother, and since he had to act as the "man of the house," he gave her extra money when he could for coal and groceries. Although he saved his money carefully, he also spent some of it for things that interested him. He spent an entire week's salary to subscribe to *Harper's Weekly* magazine for a year, and he bought ice cream frequently.

As his salary increased, George took French lessons and began to study the flute. But he soon decided that he had no musical talent, and he turned his attention for the first time to photography. At first he bought photographs that he admired. But after he went to work for another insurance firm and began making thirty-five dollars a month, he felt he could afford to take up his real interest, picture-making.

In 1871, he bought almost a hundred dollars' worth of lenses and other equipment and arranged with a local photographer to teach him the "art of photography" in his studio. As he studied the techniques, the chemicals and equipment used to develop and print photographs, he began a lifelong fascination with the art. He read every piece of literature on the subject that he could find, and he was soon out taking his own pictures at every opportunity. It required a backpack and a wheelbarrow to haul his equipment to whatever outdoor scene he wanted to photograph.

"But in those days, one did not 'take' a camera"; Eastman recalled later in an interview. "One accompanied the outfit, of which the camera was only a part. I bought an outfit and learned that it took not only a strong but also a dauntless man to be an outdoor photographer. My layout, which included only the essentials, had in it a camera about the size of a soap box, a tripod, which was strong and heavy enough to support a bungalow, a big plate-holder, a dark-tent, a nitrate bath, and a container for water. The glass plates were not in the holder ready for use; they were what is known as 'wet plates'—that is, glass that had to be coated with collodion and then sensitized with nitrate of silver in the field just before exposure. Hence the nitrate of silver was something that always had to go along, and it was perhaps the most awkward companion imaginable on a journey. Being corrosive, its container had to be of glass and the cover tight—for silver nitrate is not a liquid to get intimate with. The first time that I took a silver bath away with me, I wrapped it with exceeding great care and put it in my trunk. The cover leaked, the nitrate got out, and stained most of my clothing.

"I went out taking photographs whenever I could, read everything that was written on the subject, and generally tried to put myself on the plane of the professional photographer without, however, any idea of going into the business of photography. Since I took my views mostly outdoors—I had no studio—the bulk of the paraphernalia worried me. It seemed that one ought to be able to carry less than a packhorse load."

One day Eastman came across an article in the

Almanac, a British photography journal, that suggested a formula for making a sensitive gelatin emulsion. The article indicated that if glass plates were coated with such an emulsion they could be used dry. Eastman had changed jobs again and was working as a bank clerk. The idea in the article excited him so much that he had trouble concentrating on his work.

"The English article started me in the right direction," he recalled later. "I began in my spare time—for I was still working in the bank—to compose an emulsion that could be coated and dried on the glass plate and retain its properties long enough to be used in the field and thus avoid lugging around the dark-tent and silver nitrate bath. My first results did not amount to much, but I finally came upon a coating of gelatin and silver bromide that had all the necessary photographic qualities. . . . At first I wanted to make photography simpler merely for my own convenience, but soon I thought of the possibilities of commercial production."

Eastman had been experimenting at night, sometimes all night long, while still working at the bank. Sundays were the only days he had to catch up on his sleep, and he became thinner as the weeks went by. But his worn-out look didn't reveal the happiness and excitement he was feeling as he worked to perfect his idea. What he wanted to do now was give up his job at the bank and go into business. He would make and sell dry plates coated with his emulsion. They would be a big improvement over the wet plates in use, because photographers wouldn't have to carry the equipment needed for the wet plates.

Enthusiastically, he wrote to his uncle, Horace Eastman, asking him if he would invest in his business, providing the capital it would take to get started. His uncle turned him down. Disappointed but not crushed, he decided to start the business on a part-time basis while continuing to work at the bank. He bought more photographic materials, mixed and cooked his own emulsions in his mother's kitchen, coated the plates, took his own pictures, developed the negatives, and made his own prints.

By June 1879, he was making plates that were successful. Perhaps even more importantly, he had designed and built a machine or apparatus for coating the plates more evenly than could be done by hand. "Nobody will coat plates by hand after they have seen this machine," he declared.

At this time England was the center of photographic activity in the world, and Eastman decided he wanted to patent his invention there. He withdrew four hundred dollars from his savings account and bought a ticket to that country on a passenger ship. On July 22, 1879, he received his first patent from the British government. Then he hurried home to continue with his new business.

In September of that year, he filed for a patent with the U.S. Patent Office. By now he had engaged a patent attorney to represent him, and the attorney quickly made preparations to register the patent in France, Germany and Belgium.

In his application to the U.S. Patent Office, he wrote: "In the preparation of gelatin dry plates, great difficulty has heretofore been encountered in spreading the gelatin emulsion evenly over the glass. This has ordinarily been accomplished by a glass rod, the action of which was assisted by moving the plates slightly in different directions, causing the emulsion to flow toward the edges. It has been found difficult by this means to cover the margins of the glass or to secure an even coating on the whole surface, while the process of coating the plates in this way was necessarily slow and tedious, and therefore expensive.

"By my uniform process, plates are covered with a perfectly uniform coating of gelatin emulsion, extending entirely out to the edges of the plates, and this result is accomplished very much more rapidly than inferior plates are produced by the old method."

The following April, he was granted patent Number 226,503 for his "Method and Apparatus for Coating Plates for Use in Photography." It was the patent that launched his remarkable career, and the one for which he was inducted into the National Inventors Hall of Fame many years later.

He went to work immediately to improve the machine and his emulsions. Like Thomas Edison, who tested thousands of filaments for his electric light, Eastman tested his emulsions over and over again, trying to make improvements.

In April 1880, he leased the third floor of a large building in Rochester to set up his manufacturing business. The time was drawing close for him to launch his operations, and he worked feverishly on many things at once. He also found time to invent a new coating machine, radically different from the first one. "It is not expensive to make, simple, easy to clean," he wrote a business acquaintance. "It works as rapidly as anything heretofore devised and is adjustable to any size plate. In short, it is an eminently practical apparatus for everyone who uses emulsion in large or small quantities."

Eastman sold the British rights to his patent for the first machine, but quickly applied for a patent in that country on the second one. It was time to let the world know about his business plans, and he wrote to the largest photography merchant in New York City: "My formula is in very excellent condition and has been thoroughly tested through the hot weather both as regards manufacture and manipulation of the plates. I am also supplied with a stock of tested chemicals. Therefore, I shall be prepared to commence manufacture as soon as my laboratory is fitted up, it being almost complete at this time . . .

"The capacity of my works will be somewhat limited at first, but with the aid of recently perfected apparatus and machinery will be capable of rapid expansion if the demand requires it."

A few days before Thanksgiving, 1880, just

three years after he had become seriously interested in photography, Eastman went into operation in his own business. His laboratory was ready. He had labels and developing directions printed, and boxes for shipping the plates were made. A firm believer in advertising and salesmanship, he wrote to the New York merchant: "As soon as details of manufacturing are fully systematized, I shall advertise extensively in all the photo-journals and put competent operators on the road to demonstrate the working of the plates."

By now, Eastman had made something of a name for himself among people connected with photography. Professional photographers praised the quality of his prints and negatives, calling them "the best dry plate work on the market," and the Smithsonian Institution inquired about his work. Photography journals published articles about his inventions.

Still living at his mother's house, Eastman became acquainted with one of her boarders, Colonel Henry Strong. He was a wealthy partner in a buggy whip manufacturing business, and he enjoyed sitting on the front porch and discussing George's business plans. At first he was only an interested observer, but he was so impressed with the young inventor's confidence that he decided to invest money and become a partner in the new business. It was the start of a long and friendly business relationship between the two men. Strong gave the younger man much business advice at this early stage, and Eastman learned fast.

He established four guiding principles for his business at the outset:

1. *Production in large quantities by machinery*
2. *Low prices to increase the usefulness of the products*
3. *Foreign as well as domestic distribution*
4. *Extensive advertising and selling by demonstration.*

The business got off to a fast start. As the orders came in increasing numbers, Eastman hired more workers. Soon he had shipped thousands of his dry glass plates to wholesalers. Then the roof seemed to fall in. Suddenly, he started getting complaints from photographers that the Eastman plates had lost their sensitivity to light. Eastman hurried to his largest New York City wholesale customer, who had thousands of the plates on hand, and tested some of them. He discovered something that was then unknown: that time dulls the sensitivity of photographic emulsion. The plates stocked in the wholesaler's warehouse were now worthless.

Eastman felt he had no choice but to recall all the plates and send new ones to replace them. This would cost so much that it would nearly put him out of business, but if he didn't do it, his reputation would be ruined. Back at his shop, the young inventor tried again and again to produce a lasting emulsion with the material he had, but his efforts failed. Neither his own formula nor any other worked after more than four hundred attempts. For weeks, the factory was closed as Eastman doggedly pursued his experiments. He was so worried that he was unable to sleep, and he lay awake night after night, wondering where he had gone wrong.

Finally, the search showed that the trouble was caused by a supply of gelatin received from a manufacturer. It was not due to the Eastman formula or to his machines. Eastman had his first good night's sleep in weeks, then started operations again with a new supply of gelatin. From now on, he declared, he would test samples of every chemical or ingredient before he purchased a supply.

By now, Eastman was in debt for the first time in his life. He had to pay off some debts quickly, and this gave stimulus to the speed with which he resumed shipments to customers. But business picked up again soon, and he was able to pay off his debts and close the company's first fiscal year with a profit. He plowed the profit back into new machinery, chemicals and experiments, because he had a dream of a much larger business in the future.

Eastman's dry plate system had undoubtedly made photography easier than the wet plate system it replaced. There was less equipment to carry around now, but nevertheless, cameras were still bulky and glass plates were heavy and fragile.

As he thought about the future, Eastman concentrated on the question, "What could take the place of glass?" Other inventors had thought about this before, but no one had done very much about it.

George Eastman in his late teens. At this stage of his life he had not yet become interested in photography. Forced to leave school at fourteen because of family poverty, he became a messenger boy and then a bank clerk. (Photo courtesy of Eastman Kodak Company)

This drawing shows the cumbersome equipment and supplies a photographer had to take with him in the 1870s. Pictures were taken on glass plates, which had to be coated with liquid silver nitrate just before exposure. The inconvenience of this system is what caused George Eastman to experiment with dry plates and, later, with film. (Photo courtesy of Eastman Kodak Company)

While experimenting with film, George Eastman took this self-portrait in 1884. By this time he had already built a successful photography business selling dry plates for cameras. (Photo courtesy of Eastman Kodak Company)

By the 1890s, George Eastman's Eastman Kodak Company was supplying a complete film processing and printing service to mail-order customers. The lightweight Kodak cameras and film made photography possible for everyone. (Photo courtesy of Eastman Kodak Company)

Although George Eastman became an immensely wealthy and successful businessman with little time for experiments, he liked to take a personal hand in his shops from time to time. (Photo courtesy of Eastman Kodak Company)

Two great inventors worked together to make motion pictures a practical entertainment form. George Eastman, left, invented a flexible movie film for use in the motion picture cameras and projectors invented by Thomas Edison, right. (Photo courtesy of Eastman Kodak Company)

A lighter, less fragile and flexible substitute for glass could revolutionize cameras and photography. It was a good theory, but it needed someone who could make a practical product.

Eastman began thinking about collodion, a gelatinlike material that he had used in combination with other ingredients for his plate coatings. He had experience in handling and mixing this material, and he started to experiment with variations of it again—this time, as a substitute for glass plates. If a sort of film could be made to capture the image through a camera lens, it would be much lighter than glass.

Eastman described his experiments later in a letter to one of his attorneys: "I first conceived the process of making transparent film by coating a support with a solution of nitro cellulose, and then coating it with emulsion and afterward stripping it off—early in the year 1884. During the first half of that year I made many experiments in which I used both paper and glass as a temporary support. I used ordinary soluble gun cotton dissolved in concentrated sulphuric ether and grain alcohol equal parts, ten grains of cotton to the ounce of solvent. I sometimes added a small quantity of castor oil to the solution in order to give it more body. I coated this solution first on glass, prepared by rubbing with talc. I then poured on the glass as much of the solution of nitro cellulose as it would hold in a level position and allowed it to dry.

"I was unable with one coating to get a sufficiently heavy skin or pellicle to serve as the final support for the emulsion, so I poured on top of the first coating a solution of rubber in benzine. After drying, I poured on another portion of nitro cellulose solution and let that dry. I repeated these successive coatings eight or ten times, endeavoring to get sufficient body to the pellicle.

"I also made experiments by using paper as a *temporary* support and coating the cellulose immediately upon the paper, and afterwards coated it with the emulsion. I had no difficulty in stripping the cellulose from the paper; the cellulose adhered to the emulsion and separated from the paper. The pellicle was not heavy enough to form a reliable final support for the emulsion. I investigated various publications, endeavoring to find a method for making a thick-enough solution of cellulose in order to get a thicker coating, but I was unable to find any directions for obtaining a solution containing more than ten to twelve grains to the ounce. The experiments that I made produced films upon which I was able to make pictures by leaving the films upon the paper support during the exposure and development, and stripping them afterwards."

This description in Eastman's own words gives an idea of the patient, continuous efforts an inventor has to make as he works toward a goal. By the time he had finished his exhaustive experiments, he had invented photographic film in a continuous strip. It was the first of its kind. Without it, there would be no lightweight cameras or movies today.

Eastman filed for a patent on his film in March of 1884, then went right to work to design a mechanism to hold the film in the camera. Working with an assistant named William Walker, he produced a roll holder, a lightweight frame that could be fitted to the back of a camera. A continuous roll of the film could be fastened to the spools and wound from one to the other, just as is done in most of today's cameras. He designed the film holder so that it could be adapted to the glass-plate cameras already on the market. This was an important and necessary step if he was to get people to buy the new film, but he was already thinking about future possibilities. With film, there would be no need for the heavy, cumbersome cameras then being made. Film would open up the possibility of entirely new, lightweight cameras that could be made inexpensively. And there could be further advances in the film.

The "stripping film" which he had invented was made of a paper base, a layer of cellulose or collodion, a sensitized gelatin emulsion, and a soluble layer of gelatin between the paper and the collodion, so that this layer could be softened by warm water and the paper base separated from the negative. The negative could then be printed. Eventually, a film would be made by Eastman that wouldn't require the paper base, but for now, the new flexible film promised a revolution in photography.

By this time, Eastman had moved his operations to a four-story building at 343 State Street in Rochester—the same address used by the headquarters of the Eastman Kodak Company today. While Eastman was a shy, modest man in his social life, he was a confident and aggressive businessman. He knew his business was going to grow, and to raise more money, he formed a corporation and sold shares to investors. With fourteen shareholders, the new corporation was named the Eastman Dry Plate and Film Company. His friend, Henry Strong, was president and George Eastman was listed as treasurer. The new company opened a sales office in London, the first of many international offices to follow. The corporation had a total of $200,000 invested in it, which gave Eastman the large amount of money he needed to develop new products and make the business grow. He would need all this money and much more to reach the goal he was beginning to dream about: photography for *everyone*.

Up to this point, photography was so expensive that it was generally limited to professionals. It was a very costly hobby for amateurs, and the great majority of people did not engage in it. Eastman's two main achievements so far—the dry glass plate and the flexible paper-backed film—had been aimed at the small segment of the population who were professional photographers. But he began to see that there weren't enough of these people to buy his new film; not enough to create the big business he was dreaming about. He once said, "When we started out with our scheme of film photography, we expected that everybody who used glass plates would take up films, but we found that the number who did so was relatively small, and in order to make a large business we would have to reach the general public."

And why not, he thought. Why should photography be limited to professionals? He considered himself an amateur photographer, and he felt there must be millions more people who would be interested in taking pictures if it were simple enough and inexpensive enough. It would require a smaller, simpler camera and a flexible film that was even better than the paper-backed film he was producing now. The main drawback of the film was that the grain of the paper sometimes showed up in the negative. If he could make a transparent film strong enough to do away with the paper backing, he could eliminate this problem.

The first thing he did in tackling the film project was to get some trained help. He didn't have the time to conduct all the experiments himself, as he had in past years, because he was too busy running his business. Even though he hadn't been able to get much formal education for himself, Eastman believed in the value of a good education. What he wanted now was a college-educated research scientist to help in the development of the new film he had in mind. By hiring such a person in 1886, Eastman became one of the first American businessmen to employ a full-time research scientist. He was soon deeply involved with this scientist in work on the new film.

At the same time, he was working on the other

part of his idea: a smaller, simpler camera for the general public. In June, 1888, he had it ready. Keeping in mind his goal of selling his products in many different countries, Eastman searched for a trademark name for his new camera. He wanted a short word that could be spelled easily and pronounced in any language. Sitting down with a pencil and paper, he thought of all the combinations of letters he could. He wanted to invent a new name, one that somebody else didn't already have. He had always liked the letter "K" and he concentrated on letter combinations beginning and ending with "K." Finally, he came up with "Kodak." It was so simple that anyone could say it, no matter what their language, and it didn't mean anything else, in any language.

The new Kodak camera was a box type, light and small. It was sold to customers for twenty-five dollars, including a roll of paper-backed stripping film long enough for a hundred exposures, as well as a case and a shoulder strap. With Eastman's system, the owner sent his camera to Rochester when the film had been used up. The exposed film was removed at the factory, developed and printed, and a new one was inserted. Then the camera was shipped back to the owner. The charge for all this was ten dollars. What Eastman had done was create a whole new system of photography, not just a revolutionary camera.

He advertised the new Kodak camera and system in all the leading magazines of the time. He wanted a simple slogan for his ads that would tell people quickly what the advantages of Kodak were, and he finally came up with this: "Kodak cameras. You press the button—We do the rest." The advertising campaign was an immediate success, for it assured people that they didn't have to be experts to enjoy photography.

Meanwhile, Eastman and his research chemist were working on the project to get rid of the paper backing for film. In 1889, they succeeded in making the first transparent Eastman film. It was made by spreading a solution of nitro cellulose on a glass table two hundred feet long and nearly four feet wide. When the solution dried, it was first coated with a layer of silicate of soda to make the emulsion stick to it, and then it was coated with gelatin emulsion. It was transparent and grainless, and it could remain as the permanent support for the negative, so paper was no longer needed.

Now, Eastman knew he had the key to the revolution in photography he had envisioned. He soon found that the revolution went even further than he had anticipated. In addition to making a whole series of new cameras possible, it also was the key to something entirely new: the motion picture. Thomas Edison had been experimenting with the motion picture, and when he heard about Eastman's new flexible roll film it opened up the opportunity he had been looking for. He wrote to Eastman and requested supplies of his new film. Using this film as the basis, he went on to perfect the movie camera and projector. Eastman helped him by designing the exact type of film he needed, including the kind with sprocket holes that came to be used universally by the motion picture industry. In the following years, as the movie industry grew, Eastman supplied most of the film the studios needed.

In 1891, Eastman further improved his transparent film for Kodak cameras by designing spools for it. The film was wound onto a spool at the factory and sold separately from the camera. The customer could load it into his camera by winding the end of the film onto another spool, just as is done with many of today's cameras. This meant that the camera no longer had to be sent to Rochester for the film to be developed and new film added. Eastman shipped rolls of film to distributors everywhere, and soon stores were selling them in nearly every city and town in the country. The film no longer had to be loaded into the camera in a darkroom, but could be loaded in daylight.

Eastman was quick to follow up on the popularity of the new film. By 1890, his company was selling seven different styles and sizes of cameras, including a folding model, which had a collapsible bellows between the lens and the film. The bellows could be folded up so the camera was a slim, flat object. In the next decade, several more models were introduced, each smaller and lighter than previous cameras. Eastman called these "Pocket Kodak Cameras," and indeed, they were much smaller and lighter than anyone had dreamed of years before. In

1900, he came out with the first "Kodak Brownie," a simple camera intended for children, which sold for only one dollar. Adults bought the camera, too, because it was the best bargain that had ever been offered in photography. The film used by this camera sold for only fifteen cents a roll.

After that, the business started by George Eastman simply never stopped growing. Over the years, he kept building ever-larger factories to produce the film and cameras that the public demanded. Kodak's popularity spread to Europe, then around the world. Thousands of workers were added to Eastman's payroll. The corporation was reorganized, and then reorganized again as it grew, always with Eastman in charge. His personal fortune grew into the millions, and then a hundred million dollars.

None of this wealth seemed to change George Eastman much. He was still an amateur photographer and inventor at heart, even though he ran a multi-million dollar business. He never married, but continued to live with his mother in a fine home he had purchased in Rochester. His wealth did enable him to take annual trips to Europe, where he bought many pieces of art for his home. Most of all, he enjoyed camping trips in the wilderness with friends. Eastman liked to do the cooking on these trips; he was a fine cook who measured the ingredients in his recipes as carefully as he measured the formulas in his emulsion experiments. He was shy with strangers and disliked having too much attention or honor paid to him. Ironically, there are fewer photographs of the man who popularized photography than of any other prominent man of his day.

George Eastman is known as the inventor who made a greater fortune than almost any other—and then gave it all away. He began early, by sharing his profits with his employees. Eastman believed that for mutual success, employees should have more than just good wages. He was far ahead of management thinking at the time, for he believed that this would result in greater loyalty and better production for his company.

He began planning for "dividends on wages" for his employees when his company was still young and struggling. His first act, in 1898, was to distribute a large sum of his own money, an outright gift, to each person who worked for him. Later he set up a "wage dividend" in which each employee received money over and above his wages, based on the amount of dividend the company stock paid each year. Thus he shared the company's earnings with the people who worked there. In 1919, he gave one third of his own holdings of company stock, then worth ten million dollars, to his employees. He was also among the first industrialists to establish "fringe benefits" such as retirement pensions, life insurance and disability insurance for employees.

Eastman didn't just throw away his money carelessly. He gave careful thought to the things he wanted to accomplish by giving away money. And he didn't do it for publicity or fame. For example, he admired the Massachusetts Institute of Technology, a fine engineering college, because he had hired some of its graduates and they had become his best assistants. He gave a total of twenty million dollars to M.I.T. without letting his own name be known to the press. The gift was listed as coming from a "Mr. Smith," and M.I.T. students didn't know who the real giver was.

He was interested in the idea of dental clinics, to help great numbers of people get proper dental care. He came up with complete plans and financial backing for a two-and-a-half million dollar dental clinic for Rochester, and offered care to all the children of that city. When he was asked why he favored dental clinics, he replied, "I get more results for my money than in any other philanthropic scheme. It is a medical fact that children can have a better chance in life with better looks, better health and more vigor if the teeth, nose, throat and mouth are taken care of at the crucial time of childhood." These were the reasons he also gave dental clinics to London, Paris, Rome, Brussels and Stockholm.

Remembering his poverty-stricken childhood, when music and flowers were not available, he became interested in these things, too. Although he had long since decided he didn't have a talent for music, he enjoyed the beauty of it. Anxious that other people have the opportunity to enjoy this beauty, he worked out a plan for a great school of music, a theater and a symphony orchestra for Rochester. As a result, that city has had a fine symphony orchestra for years. He also supported the creation of a medical school and hospital for the University of Rochester. One day in 1924, he signed away thirty million dollars to the University of Rochester, M.I.T., Hampton and Tuskegee Institutes. "Now I feel better," he said.

By the time George Eastman died in 1932, he had given away his entire fortune. He also willed his Rochester home to become a museum of photography, which it now is. Raised in poverty, he appreciated money for what it could do, but he cared little about keeping it for himself.

This "amateur photographer," as he called himself, changed photography for all time. By his inventive genius he simplified it, so that anyone can take pictures with a handheld camera, simply by pressing a button. He made photographers of us all. Furthermore, he broadened the scope of photography, so that it became a wonderful means of teaching and spreading knowledge.

In medical research, the camera has become the "companion piece to the microscope." Time-lapse motion pictures taken at intervals of minutes or hours speed up on the screen for observation of cancer cell division. The sensitive electrocardiograph gives a photographic record of heart functionings. The X-ray film, which George Eastman developed, is used daily around the world to diagnose illnesses.

In science and industry, the camera is the recording eye for observation and measurement. With photography, scientists can explore and measure the light along the surface of the sun, estimate the amount of ozone in the earth's atmosphere, and determine wind velocities or the time and place of a distant earthquake. It will show the groupings of atoms in steel or silk, or discover the mystery of elasticity in a rubber band or a watch spring. X-ray machines can probe into and inspect the cross-section of an airplane's structural parts against flaws.

Photography affects our lives in so many ways today that we seldom think about it. We owe most of this progress to the remarkable revolution that George Eastman brought about. As one historian put it, "It was a revolution of enormous importance to the world, brought about by the devotion of a bank clerk amateur." George Eastman would like that description.